Skating On Thin Ice

Skating On Thin Ice

Ann Terry

with

Thelma Sangster

Pickering Paperbacks

First published in 1985
by Pickering & Inglis,
3 Beggarwood Lane,
Basingstoke, Hants RG23 7LP,
United Kingdom

ISBN: 0 7208 0657 7

Text set by Ann Buchan (Typesetters), Surrey
Reproduced, printed and bound in Great Britain by
Hazell Watson & Viney Limited,
Member of the BPCC Group,
Aylesbury, Bucks

Contents

Acknowledgements

There are many people I would like to thank, especially
– my mother, Evelyn Terry, who bought me my first pair
of skates
–   Pastor Ken and Heather Blackwell, Bertha and Floyd
Agar and Pastor Conrad D'Friese who taught me so much
about the Christian life
– Clarice and Dennis Pailthorpe, Valerie Moon-Barnes
and Michael Barnes, Diane Thomas, Judith Wilson and
Dorothy Megham, my very dear friends
– Thelma Sangster for her patient and thorough work
– Gerald Williams for finding time to read the manuscript
and write a foreword for it.
    Without the encouragement and love of all these, and
many others, this book would not have been written.

Ann Terry
January 1985

Foreword
by Gerald Williams

Ann Terry is someone who has flitted in and out of my crowded life in recent years, usually when we have been brought into contact through the organisation 'Christians in Sport'. I meet all sorts of people that way: professional footballers, tennis players (mainly, I suppose), cricketers, badminton players. . . . Ann is the only Christian ice skater I've met, though.

My experience of her world is hardly even sketchy – the Lake Placid Winter Olympics, and people I met there as I reported for the BBC on the gold medal triumph of Robin Cousins.

So it is not just Ann Terry but the whole travelling menagerie of the ice skating world that I have learned about in reading her manuscript. The names are different, but the scenario is much the same, it seems to me, on, say, the tennis circuit: life in a suitcase, transient acquaintances, excitements that don't last, empty hotel rooms that have to be endured, mountain peaks that never, in reality, have the breathless thrill you had anticipated. New cities, strange currency, different languages, recurring situations which, before very long, simply do not fulfil. Ann puts it this way: 'I had been too busy chasing what lay round the next corner, or at the end of the rainbow. But now I knew: the answer was that nothing lay there.'

Like many of us in sport, Ann found her answer when she cried out to God. Almost everyone does at some time or another, and those in whose heart a deep faith in Jesus springs to life have no other impulse than to spread the

Good News that is for everyone – if only they will lay aside their misunderstandings and prejudices and listen!

Ann Terry is spilling over with the desire to share the power that has changed her life and given it *lasting* delight. Her book is a major step: Ann going public.

May God guard her and inspire her.

1: Hello World!

'Half an hour to curtain up!' The call from Peter, stage manager of the Pavilion Theatre, Skegness, sent panic signals through the dressing room, where I and eight other girl skaters with Gerald Palmer's Summer Ice Carnival were getting into costume for our opening number.

We stood one behind the other, each girl deftly hooking the back fastenings of the checked dress in front of her. In four months of working together we had learned the short cuts.

'Ann, are you decent? Can I come in?' My partner, Johnny, was outside the door.

'Yes, come in' – we answered in chorus.

Johnny stepped into the room, tall and slim in his blue denims and loud check shirt. He carried a bunch of fresh flowers – and a wrapped box.

'I'm going to miss you, partner,' and he held out the flowers and the box.

I took his gifts and kissed him lightly on the cheek, so as not to smudge our thick stage make-up. 'I'm going to miss you too. . . .'

'Oh Johnny. . . .'

Tears stung my eyes, and I took a grip on myself. I was leaving the show, leaving England. It was altogether too late for regrets. The future waited.

Inside the box was a neat little cowboy doll, dressed Oklahoma-style. 'Gee thanks, partner . . . it'll remind me of you.'

George Miller, one of the solo stars, was the next to poke his head round the door. He carried a red velvet cushion on which sat a genie with a lamp, representing one of his favourite numbers. I was touched. The show was like family, and people in it cared for each other.

'Fifteen minutes. . .' That voice was implacable, winding us up for a performance which was timed to run like clockwork. There was a feverish scramble in front of the mirror where girls were touching up their hair.

'Annie, lass. You've got my red bonnet on.' My Scottish friend, Betty was tugging at the ribbons.

'Oh, sorry. . . Where's the blue one?' I pulled my wandering thoughts back to the urgency of the moment.

Someone thrust the blue bonnet at me. Cramming it over my dark brown, curly hair, which had earned me the title 'Buzby Bonks' at school, I examined the effect critically in the light from the staring bulbs around the dressing room mirror.

A face looked back at me, washed-out in spite of the sun-tan coloured make-up. I had forgotten to put on any eye-liner and false lashes. Without them I would look expressionless in the strong lights out front. Quickly I remedied the omission, brushing some extra black onto my eyelashes, wishing my heart would stop pounding, as if it were in a race.

Out in the theatre we could hear the orchestra tuning up as the audience found their seats. The show was a popular attraction for holidaymakers, who were generally a delight to play to, since they came in a frame of mind to enjoy themselves. Professional skating is a magical spectacle of fun and artistry, and it certainly appealed to the friendly Yorkshire families, the sprinkling of Scottish folk, and Americans from the nearby base who were in Skegness that summer. There were never any problems filling the seats during our run.

Tonight a cold lump of nervous apprehension had settled in the pit of my stomach and I clutched the edge of the dressing table for support. That face, now looking back at me with sparkling eyes, that figure dressed to suggest a country girl from Oklahoma – they masked the ordinary, chattery, giggly, and often pushy person who was Ann Terry, and raised her into a fantasy symbol on which the audience could feast.

'Five minutes'. . . I pushed my feet into the stiff, white leather skating boots and fumbled with hook fastenings, all thumbs. One last check in the mirror. Seams straight? Yes, straight. All OK? Yes, OK.

'Standby!'. . . We pushed out of the dressing room and into the wings, trying not to fall over each other or any piece of stage equipment in the dim light.

Joyce, leading the chorus line whispered to Bill, the ice engineer, 'How's the ice?' We listened for his answer, 'Good and smooth,' and smiled at each other with relief. Cracks in that milky surface could treacherously launch a skater into an unexpected orbit off the small stage. Barbara, our blonde star, was still nursing a bruised leg from a spectacular landing in a big bass drum.

I side-stepped as I passed Bill . . . he was sometimes a bit too friendly to the girls.

Waiting for the curtain-up we took off our skateguards. My knees still remembered the fall when I tried to waltz into a number wearing the hard nylon guards. What does a performer do in such circumstances? Nothing but pick herself up and carry on, ice-cool outwardly, even if dead with embarrassment inside and aching in several new places. The show must go on!

'Curtain up!'. . . The mist which earlier had hung over the ice had cleared in the warmth from the brilliant overhead lights. The front of the stage was marked with coloured lamps. Spotlights swept the stage and into the beams of magical, changing colour we danced, smiling our toothpaste smiles at an audience we could not see, and miming the song in time with the dubbers back stage, to create the illusion that we were actually singing the number. It wasn't cheating – it took all our breath to skate.

'O-o-o-h, Oklahoma where the winds come sweeping down the plain. . . . ' It was a catchy, popular song from a Broadway musical, a current London hit. The audience clapped in time to the music, and their approval reached us across the footlights.

I didn't have to think where my feet were going. The orchestra led us through our paces and with Johnny's arm round my waist I felt as if I were flying. Tall as I was he topped me by nearly a foot, and could swing me up into the air as if I were as light as a butterfly.

Turn and glide and jump; cross back, roll and swing. Kick, lift, kiss. The chorus line swung out, cut, changed partners, circled and set to partners again in fast rhythmic patterns. All kept an eye out for the edge of the stamp-sized ice rink and the sharp blades of the other skaters.

Turn, glide and soar; cross back, roll and swing; kick, lift, kiss. Goodbye Oklahoma, goodbye Skegness, hello Canada, hello great big world. . .

'O K L A H O M A. . . . O - K - L - A - H - O - M - A. . . .OKLAHOMA. . . . OKAY!' We skidded to a halt, jumping into our partners' arms on precisely the right beat, stretching legs and arms prettily, and flashing our brilliant smiles at the audience. They rewarded us with thunderous applause, and piercing whistles as the gold silk curtains swished across.

Now it was a race against the clock, with five minutes to change for the Rose Garden ballet scene. The show's two comedians took over, keeping the audience happy with their cleverly-timed patter.

I struggled awkwardly with the stiff and prickly net of my costume, wishing I was like buxom Betty, instead of being tall, lanky – and flat-chested.

The character dances suited me better. I was in my element when we blacked up and sang 'Mammee, how I love ya, how I love ya, my dear old mammee. . . .'

That number, however, had some really difficult precision steps, calling for careful synchronisation. Our choreographer Beatrice Livesay would be sure to point out any raggedness afterwards.

'Come on girls and boys. You have to do better than

this or we'll have a rehearsal after the show.' She would say it with a smile, but she sought for perfection, and would demand everything from us, even on a two-show day, when we were dropping with exhaustion, and our feet ached from carrying two pounds weight of metal and leather through eight chorus numbers in a two to three hour performance twice over.

Between numbers Gerald Palmer, the producer, sent for me. He was an impressive figure, portly, always with a cigar, and a perfect gentleman to everyone, whether they were stage hands or stars, it didn't matter.

'Ann, I want to wish you all the best and bon voyage.' He handed me an envelope which contained my salary, and then, with a flourish, produced a box of chocolates.

I thanked him for giving me the chance to skate in the show. It had not been easy to get this job. There were so many ice skaters around and I was difficult to fit into a chorus line, because of my height.

He waved his cigar expansively. 'I hope everything will go all right for you and Michael. . . .'

I took a deep breath. 'I'm still going to Canada, but I think the wedding's off.'

'Ann, you're a good line skater. Morris Chalfen is always looking for top line skaters – and I'd recommend you any day. Just write to me if things don't work out.'

I was speechless. Morris Chalfen, the big impresario of Holiday on Ice, USA! Had I heard aright? Only the cream of skaters made it into that show. Dreamily I wrote some imaginary bold, black headlines for the Brighton Evening Argus . . . 'Skater Ann Terry makes the big time'.

Music called me out of my daydream, back to the next number, Autumn Leaves. I smoothed down my well-worn leaves and hoped the patches weren't visible to the audience. In fact those costumes looked super under the lights. But that was theatre for you. A world of illusion and make-believe to lift people out of their worries for an hour or two.

We were young and may have seemed carefree, gliding

13

across the blue-white square of ice as if set free from the pull of the earth. That too was an illusion. We had heartaches and worries about money, the price of digs, broken marriages, unhappy home lives, our futures, just like everyone else. A skater's life was hard and chancy, whether we were at the bottom or the top.

The final curtain rang down to a mighty burst of applause. We stood, with genuine smiles pinned to our faces, as bouquets were handed to the stars. There was the stilts skater, whose wife was the juggler. Barbara took hers: she had well deserved it. Irene from Brighton came next, then Rosemary, the main singer. Beatrice took a special bow and was awarded a bouquet too.

After the show, we had a party in the Green Room. I was leaving, and if we needed another excuse it was Saturday night. Skaters are sociable beings and always ready to find a reason for a celebration.

I got my bouquet at the party, we had champagne, sandwiches and cakes, and I was showered with presents. Everyone kissed me, and tried to encourage me to go through with marrying Michael.

'I had cold feet before my wedding,' said Audrey, the redhead. 'But it was all right in the end.'

'You've got a good guy there, paying your way like that,' said Evie, who dated Americans from a nearby base and knew how to get what she wanted.

The evening ended with a rather raucous round of 'Auld Lang Syne' and 'For She's a Jolly Good Fellow'. The comics were the worse for wear, and Dawn was tearful, not on my account, I felt, having seen how she'd been tipping it down.

There was another round of kissing at parting. I no longer tried to hide the tears. What a wonderful bunch of troupers they were, generous to newcomers like me and with little of the backstage bickerings and jealousies associated with temperamental show-biz folk.

'Goodbye Ann, goodbyeee . . . be sure and write.' The voices trailed away as Joyce and Betty and I set out to walk to our digs in Drummond Road, carrying flowers and presents, plus skates, rehearsal gear and make-up box.

Mrs Parker was still up and came out from her warm kitchen. 'Would you like a cocoa, ducks?'

"Quack, quack,' I murmured under my breath for Joyce and Betty's benefit, and we giggled. Aloud I said 'Yes please,' and followed her into the kitchen, which smelt delicious from her evening's baking. She plonked down on the kitchen table some of her latest batch of cakes and while we munched she questioned us about the performance.

It was a nightly ritual. Mrs Parker took a motherly interest in her guests, and her visitors book included names of many now famous stage personalities, whom she had accommodated when they were less prominent.

'I see you got some presents, ducky.' She took the flowers and found a vase to keep them fresh.

'Yes, have a look.' We gossiped about the party and about Gerald Palmer's promise.

'Looks as if you'll be all right then.' She gave me a peck on the cheek and pushed a comforting hot water bottle into my arms. 'Goo'night, love. What time do you want waking? Harry'll help you with your luggage in the morning.'

In my room I opened the brown envelope Gerald Palmer had given me. Bless his heart, he had slipped me an extra five pounds. That was a lot of money – enough to buy me a new dress on the other side of the water. For this all but penniless, twenty-year-old, prospective world traveller that was a bonus indeed.

2: The Great Escape

Packing when I was leaving England for good (I hoped) was a nightmare operation. I muddled about for the next two days, trying to squeeze everything into my trunks and cases, much to the exasperation of my mother and aunt, who were supervising.

'Ann, you don't need to take all that waste paper,' Mum said looking at my files of correspondence.

'Oh Mum, I have to keep in touch with all my friends.' The packing was constantly being interrupted by the phone. School chums, Jack Arlidge from the *Evening Argus* sports desk, and skating friends from Blackpool and Brighton shows wanted to wish me good luck.

There was a shower of letters and telegrams. Two that gave me some comfort were from Michael who was going to pick me up at Toronto train station and Gigi, my pen pal, who would meet me as the ship docked at Montreal.

'I wish I could go with you,' said Mum. She had been to Canada once for a holiday, and had often said she'd like us all to go out there and live. Dad, however, wasn't the travelling type, especially when he was promoted to foreman at Greenfields, the removal firm for which he worked.

On 21st September, 1959 I left 138, Trafalgar Road, Portslade. Mother broke down at Portslade Station and Father said gruffly, 'God bless you and take care. Keep in touch.' Pat and Jill my two younger sisters shouted as the train pulled out, 'We'll come and join you.'

I waved out of the window until they disappeared from

view. If I had been alone I might have wept too, but Dorothy my school chum was coming with me as far as Victoria. There she handed me over to Bill Bean, a friend I'd met in Jersey that year. He took me in his private taxi-cab, with my three trunks, two suitcases and a small vanity case (together with a celebration bottle of champagne, a present from Bill) to Euston, where we loaded ourselves onto the boat train for Liverpool.

A few hours later I stood on the passenger deck of the Cunard ship, Corinth, clutching the half-empty champagne bottle. Streamers and flowers fluttered between us and the shore, as the great ship pulled away from the dock. I felt utterly desolate and alone in the jubilant crowd.

My cabin companions were three elderly ladies. More grey heads greeted me at the dining table. Weren't there any young people on board?

There were and I found them in the ballroom that night, and around the keep fit sessions, swimming pool, deck games and the cinema. That ship was organised like a high-class holiday village, and I soon began to feel my usual happy self.

We made good time till we hit a storm two days out which delayed the ship by an extra day. I was one of the few good sailors among the passengers, and rode out the storm with unimpaired appetite. All the activities were cancelled, a state of affairs I set about remedying. I routed out the band, who were 'resting' at the bar, and persuaded them to help me run a dance for the passengers who were upright. About thirty hardy young souls gathered in the second-class ballroom prepared to be entertained.

Rock-and-roll was the rage in the UK. So, while the ship rolled through the storm we rocked across the sloping dance floor to the tune of 'Green Door', falling into the band and out again, to screams of laughter, having what one might call a whale of a time.

Up on deck during the storm I was enchanted to meet Mr and Mrs Wride from Suffolk who were in their

17

seventies, but on honeymoon. We got into conversation and I told them about Michael, and how he had opened the way for me to go to Canada.

'It's like a fairy story. I've always wanted to travel, since I was three. My father's really responsible. He started me collecting stamps. To their looks of surprise I explained how in the removal business it was easy to collect foreign stamps. People wrote from abroad about their furniture or luggage. Once dad had been given a whole album stuffed with stamps.

'Stamps are wonderful,' I went on. 'You can learn the history and geography of countries, and all about nature and the costumes, and the people who have done wonderful things. All those little pictures. I wanted to travel and see those places.'

The Wrides burst out laughing. 'We believe you,' they said.

Mr Wride looked a little concerned at the few pounds I had with me.

'Twenty pounds won't take you very far, Ann,' he said. 'You'd better come down to the purser's office so we can check on the current rate of exchange.'

'I've got someone meeting me, and anyway I hope to get a job.' I said it with a great deal more conviction than I felt. How would I make out? I hadn't thought much beyond meeting Michael. But the natural optimism of youth wouldn't allow me to worry for long. 'Everything's going to be all right,' I told myself. After all, hadn't I managed to pull off the great escape from Portslade successfully?

Standing on the swinging deck, watching the horizon roll from side to side I thought back over the years to my first class at the Tony Martin School of Dancing in Hove. Then the stage shows at St Barnabas Church Hall, Hove. How I longed to become a professional dancer but already at eight years I was 5ft in height and clearly going to be too tall for ballet. I cried my eyes out, till Mother saw she had to do something to shut me up.

18

'We'll go and look at some ice skates tomorrow,' she promised. That dried my tears in an instant. I had seen my first ice show at the age of three, with Valerie Moon and Cecilia College. Later on there was Belita and Gloria Nord, who was as beautiful as an angel. It had been an introduction to fairyland, and the pictures still glowed in my memory.

Next day she took her own precious pair of unworn, white, fur-lined Canadian skating boots, which had been sent her as a gift during the war, to a shoe shop in Western Road, and sold them for enough to buy us both skating boots, though as far as I know she never wore hers. Mine were beige, a colour I disliked. However, I was duly enrolled in the children's Saturday skating club at Brighton Ice Rink, West Street. From then on my weekends were devoted to the ice, with my friend's two older sisters escorting me each Saturday.

So I grew a whole lot of new ambitions, which Mother tried to discourage when she saw how important it was all becoming to me. I don't think she wanted me to be disappointed by failure, since she knew how stiff the competition was. But she was far, far too late. The seeds of both skating and the urge to travel were sown at three.

When I was ten years old, the teacher at the club told my father, 'You should let Ann have lessons. She has real talent and could go far . . . perhaps take medals or even go into it professionally.'

Dad was taken aback and didn't know whether to believe her. 'I think she just wants the money,' he told me on the way home on the top of the bus.

'Oh, Dad, don't be like that. I'm getting better all the time,' I exclaimed.

Nothing came of it. We didn't have the money to spare. We lived in a bungalow at Stanley Avenue, Mile Oak. Dad shifted furniture for Greenfields, and the weeks he drove he got extra money, but it was still hard to make ends meet.

But a good family stands by when needs are felt. My

Auntie Win helped to pay entry fees for competitions and Nan Terry ran up my costumes. So we made headway, against odds, and determination paid off in the end. When I was eleven I competed against the other top standard ice dancers for a chance to teach some of the beginners, and got the job. This meant free time on the ice every Saturday. First I taught in the dancing club, for an hour. Then from ten o'clock to noon I was given a free session, which helped me to progress.

I worked a few little stratagems to further my career. When I noticed that people landed on two feet instead of one, doing an axle jump, I would contrive to fall beside them, and listen to what the teacher was saying to correct them. Then I put the lesson into practice.

We all worked on centring our spins, achieving dizzy speeds. We synchonised to music, and copied all the steps, jumps, spins, spirals we had seen in championship performances.

Around this time, our family moved house to Trafalgar Road, Portslade. Dad had been promoted to foreman and the house was next to the garages and warehouses. He had to be up at six o'clock in the morning to give the men their orders.

It was a huge house, with sixteen rooms and big fireplaces. Suddenly we had a few luxuries, like a TV and a telephone. But still no skating lessons. Mother and I never really discussed it, but I knew she was adamant on the subject.

Mother was very beautiful. She was only 5ft 2ins. with a good figure, striking looks and an outgoing personality. Even when we were really hard-up she managed to turn herself out with style. It must have been a blow to her that her first baby, born with a wry neck, was not the ideally beautiful child she had hoped for, and needed special care in early days.

After me came Pat and Jill. I always thought of one as cleverer, and the other as prettier than me. As I grew up I turned to Dad, who seemed to understand me. Out in the

20

shed while he repaired broken furniture and ornaments for clients, we would talk over my dreams of travelling the world as a skater.

He would never try to laugh me out of it. 'Ann, you are a doer like me. You enjoy yourself.'

One day I said, 'I'm a different person when I skate. Just like Pat plays the piano to help her with her studies so interpreting the music and making up steps sets me free from all this inner tension. . . .'

An Olympic coach once came to the ice rink. Gersch Wheeler had coached many champions to gold medals. He liked my style, but told me I had picked up a few bad habits. 'I wish I had seen you earlier. I could have found you a sponsor,' he said. I did not know whether to be encouraged or dashed.

Amateur competitions should have come next. But we didn't have the money for the coaching and the travel involved. Getting to the top was a very expensive business and only kids from rich families could afford it.

One day an Austrian coach told me: 'I want to train you.'

When I said I hadn't the money, he asked me what I could afford. I said two shillings and sixpence (Mum insisted that I save the other five shillings from my Saturday job). I was short by five whole shillings. But he accepted my two and sixpence, very generously. 'Only keep it from the others,' he warned.

Those twelve lessons helped me get an audition at Bournemouth Ice Show, when I was 14. And when I got into the show against stiff competition from all those girls whose parents could afford the expensive ice-lessons I was in seventh heaven. But the joy was short-lived. In a solo turn as the gardener in Queen of Hearts I was executing a near-perfect flying parallel spin, when I hit a piece of wood and pulled a cartilage in my right knee. As a result I was out of the show for five whole weeks and at the end of that time had to go back to Mile Oak Secondary Modern School for Girls in great disappoinment, wondering if I would ever get a chance like that again. I had been given time off school for three months, but my contract was decorated with red clauses and exemptions. One of these had come into force due to the length of my convalescence.

Rich kids I knew at Brighton had special tutors for schooling, so that they could have enough ice time when it was freer during the day. Some parents even went to the length of sending their gifted children to Switzerland and Austria to live, where the ice was plentiful and the training was of the highest standard. That was the way champions were made, who would become solo stars in the ice show world.

By the time I was due to leave school my dream of travelling the world as a professional ice skater was amounting to an obsession. How it would come about I didn't know. For one thing, in England this could only be a seasonal job, and the rest of my time I would have to earn my living at something else.

'You've got to have another string to your bow, besides skating,' said Mother in alarm. 'You'd better learn shorthand-typing. That'll stand you in good stead if the skating doesn't work out.'

So though I could have left Mile Oak at fifteen, I stayed on for another year to learn commerce, and secretarial subjects. Mother was right. It did carry me through. When I left school I became a hotel receptionist, which was seasonal, and at Christmas went into 'Dick Whittington on Ice' at Brighton. After that I worked for a solicitor, a laundry company and an engineering firm. The next Christmas I was at Blackpool's Icedrome in the 'Queen of Hearts'. This gave me the opportunity to skate in an ice show there for six months in the summer.

I began to think a lot about Canada, where, I had been told, there could be as many as eight ice rinks in one town. The ice shows travelled through the northern hemisphere in the summer, making their own ice in civic centres and other huge buildings.

Meeting Michael had given me the push I needed. Now

I was on my way to Canada, and hoped eventually, when I had sorted out my romantic affairs, to work in one of these travelling ice-shows.

I knew from experience, but didn't dwell on it, that the skater's career was a fragile one. A fall on the ice could shorten it, suddenly and dramatically. There was always the possibility of a pulled muscle, a torn ligament, broken bones, cuts and bruises and other mischances. I had known some adagio skaters who had hit a wad of chewing gum on the ice. The man, carrying his partner in an overhead lift, overbalanced and fell with her to the ground. The crash damaged his spine and broke her leg, putting them both out of work for months.

But I dismissed these unpleasant thoughts. 'I'll take my chance,' I said over the ship's rail, as if throwing a challenge to the wild sea and sky, and never thinking that in all the universe there was any being other than the wheeling gulls to take note of my brave words.

3: Windy City

Montreal at last. The Corinth edged up to the dockside and the passengers crowded to the rails to search for welcoming faces in the waiting crowd. The magnitude of the adventure swept over me, now that I was about to sever the last link with all that spelt home. What if there was no one there to meet me?

But of course there would be Gigi, my pen pal. Her Canadian voice rang in my ears from a brief call she had made to the ship, 'Look out for me. I'll be wearing a white carnation in my buttonhole and I'll be with Al. We've just got engaged.'

When we finally met on the dockside she swept me into a perfumed embrace. She was dinky in height but with a lot of personal magnetism. Al gripped my hand and said, 'Welcome Ann, to Montreal.'

They took me on a whirlwind tour of Montreal. I had a kaleidoscope impression of skyscrapers, of hustle and bustle in the streets as people shopped, though it was seven o'clock. I heard a gabble of French everywhere. The oversized cars drove on the wrong side of the street, and in the Mount Royal Hotel a high-speed lift zoomed us up to a fabulous restaurant, where we ate a gorgeous meal looking out at a stunning view.

Then they dashed me over to Gigi's home to meet her parents who tried to communicate with me in French through Gigi. 'Will you stay with us?' they asked. But I had already made plans to meet Michael at Toronto station and needed to move on my way.

'Ann, there may be a job here in the sports centre' Gigi

told me. It was very tempting, but I wanted to get things over and done with where Michael was concerned.

On the train I tried to work out what I was going to say to him. What could I say to this man, who was probably expecting me to change my mind about the wedding? Of one thing I was certain, no one, but no one was going to push me into anything like marriage, till I was ready.

I thought back to the day of our first encounter. I was working as a secretary in a Brighton engineering firm, and was on the reception desk, filling in, when I lifted my eyes and saw him pass by.

'Hello there!' he said. His deep, warm voice, and his Dirk Bogarde looks struck me instantly. I took in big brown eyes, with laughter lines at the corners, dark, curly hair, perfect teeth and romantic tan.

'Who's that?' I said to the empty desk.

I was not quite brave enough to waylay him myself so I got old Fred, a factory hand friend of mine, to take him a note, asking for a meeting at lunch time.

It was very forward of me, for those days, but he didn't seem to mind. We sat and had a sandwich out on the factory lawn while he told me about himself. He was an engineering apprentice, taking his finals in a few months' time.

We arranged to rendezvous after work. He had a car and took me home, and our happy relationship went on from there, until he announced, after his finals, that he was going to Canada. Then, he asked to marry me.

I had mixed feelings about this. One half of me wanted to keep him and yet the other side of me wanted to be free to travel and see the world. I was not ready to be tied down.

My parents liked Michael but made a condition to their acceptance of him as a son-in-law.

'If you say you want to marry Ann, you show that you love her by saving up the fare for her to join you.' I think they felt he was irresponsible where money was concerned and this would be a test of how real he was. They couldn't afford it, that was for sure, and neither could I on what I earned.

So that was how it was left, until the telegram arrived saying, 'Money on the way. Come at once.'

That had thrown me into a panic. I was ready to travel, yes, but not ready for the strings attached to the offer. So I cabled back, 'Can't accept. I do not love you. I want to travel. I wouldn't make you a good wife. Don't send money.'

However, back came a reply, 'Come anyway. Money sent.'

So, the sight of Michael waving on the other side of a dividing rope was good indeed. So was the feeling of his embrace. 'Welcome to Canada honey. I'm so glad to see you,' he said as he kissed me.

I felt the old familiar warmth of his affection for me. There was no chance of conversation however, for he quickly introduced me to his brother Derek and sister-in-law Jenny. They were to put me up.

Jenny and I chatted easily while the men got the luggage into the car and soon we were passing through Toronto, which looked a nice, clean-cut town without much of a city centre. The countryside spread itself before me. It was late fall and the rich, rust, gold colours from the maple trees were lit by the early morning sun. My heart lifted with happiness. It was a newly minted world in which it was good to be young and in love with life.

Brantford was a clean and spacious town, with open plan gardens to the fronts of the houses. There seemed to be room for everything. Would there be room for this limey?

I planned to go job-hunting the following day, but to my disappointment I found that there were none. Apparently two factories had closed and the redundant workers were taking up all the available vacancies.

I found that Mike was paying for my keep, and this embarrassed me.

'Don't let it worry you, honey,' Mike assured me. 'This situation won't last for ever.'

'I'm not giving up till I get a job,' I told him.

I did get one interview at a chemical plant but they told me there were two hundred people after this secretarial post and they would have to do a short list. I was on it. I went away to wait, not very hopefully, since it was obvious to me that local people would have priority.

At the ice rink I met the Harrisons. They taught ice skating, and I could feel their eyes on me as I spun and jumped, performing some of my fancy show steps to the music. A space had cleared around me. Other skaters were watching. Dick glided up to me and said, 'You're no beginner!'

I told him a little about myself and asked if there was any work at the ice rink. Jean had joined us by now. 'What about Mike Kirby?' she asked.

'What about him?' I countered, never having heard the name. I was soon to learn that he was really big news, being the Canadian ice champion who had set up ice rinks across Canada and the USA.

'He runs schools from Toronto to Chicago' said Dick. 'Maybe we could do something about that.'

He and Jean pulled a few strings, and soon surprised me with an offer of a job from Mike Kirby at his ice rink in Chicago!

I had to borrow the money to get there, so I cabled dear old Dad. He sent me the fifty dollars – a fortune then – and about a week later I took a plane to Chicago. Mike escorted me to the airport and we stood awkwardly together. I knew he was hurting inside, but only now did I realise how little time we had had alone together, without Jenny or his brother being present. Perhaps if we had had a little more time. . . . The lump in my throat threatened to choke me because I was really fond of him, and this was the parting of the ways.

Twenty-five years later I was to meet him again, and

know even more clearly that of all the men I ever met he was the most genuine, and the best friend a girl could have had. But our union was not to be.

I could have stayed. On that very morning phone calls had come from personnel officers in four companies who had interviewed me. All offered jobs, good ones with comfortable salaries and prospects of security. It would have meant turning my back on the world of ice skating, and opting for domesticity. I was simply not interested, but it was unsettling.

On the plane I sat next to Eileen, a friendly social worker who couldn't resist putting in a little overtime on me. When I exclaimed at the sight of Chicago spreading below like a box of jewels she frowned. 'You're asking for trouble going to Windy City alone.'

She was heading for a conference at the Hilton Hotel and she insisted that I go there with her. She gave me tea and the hotel phone number in case of emergencies. Then she put me in a taxi to the other side of town.

Mike Kirby had booked me into an apartment hotel miles away from the ice school. So my first night in Chicago was spent rattling around in three rooms and a bathroom. Fortunately they were centrally heated against the chill wind that seemed to meet one at every corner. I braved the dark streets and the cold wind to find food, for there was none in the kitchen refrigerator.

Round the corner there was a club restaurant, recommended by the hotel desk clerk. I went there to eat, a little afraid of the prices since it looked very select. But they knew nothing about making tea. They brought me a pot. I assumed it was tea and waited for it to brew up. When I poured it out it was water. The tea bag still hung on the outside of the pot. I felt I had come to a foreign land.

Louie, the restaurant owner, an affable man in a white jacket, introduced me to Hank, who, on learning I was from England, offered to take me on a tour of Chicago by night.

Louie approved. 'Hank's OK,' he said, helping me on with my coat.

We spun through the brilliantly-lit canyons of the Windy City and I learned that under this sophistication moved a dark stream of violence. Hank and I finished our tour at the Starlight Room, then he saw me to the hotel lobby.

Next morning, when I arrived at the club restaurant, I found breakfast was on the house, courtesy of Hank. He waved away my thanks. 'That's for England' he said. 'I was a GI there in the war.' Hank's last gesture was to escort me across town in his Mercedes Benz to Mike Kirby's office.

All this seemed remarkable at the time, and I tended to call it luck. Later I was to see it differently. At any rate, I still had ten dollars on me when I arrived in Mike Kirby's office.

He was a tall, elegant man with dark hair which looked permed, and he asked me to work out on the ice. I whirled around a few times but it was smaller than the Skegness ice tank. How could anyone learn properly on this? One glide and I was at the other side. I didn't dare do a flying camel for fear of hitting the wall.

'It's technique,' said Mike. 'You'll get used to it. We even have ice shows here.' He might have been sincere, but I laughed.

'Come up to the office Ann, we have to talk business.' I took off my skates and followed him.

The first shock I had was discovering that he had not applied for a work permit for me. I stared in horror. That meant I could not earn a salary, and I knew that they took weeks to process applications from abroad. They might even withhold it. In addition I had signed a declaration on entering Canada that I would stay there a year.

That wasn't all. While his secretary was out of the room getting me a drink his phone rang. His conversation was guarded but I heard enough to learn that he was filing for bankruptcy. I was in an awful spot.

When he put the phone down I said bluntly, 'Does that mean I haven't got a job here after all?'

He tried to bluff it out. 'I'll sort something out' he said. 'Go back to your hotel and I'll phone you.'

'I can't afford it. And I won't be earning a salary to pay for it.'

At that moment his Toronto manager came in, and I was asked to leave. Stunned, and with no promises from Mike I left the office and went out into the street, wondering what to do.

I used some of my meagre dollars to get a cab back to my apartment and then sat staring through the window at the other apartment blocks in the street, feeling utterly at a loss. For once my cheerfulness and optimism had deserted me.

Then a voice sounded in my head, 'If you ever need me, here's my number.' Of course, I still had a friend in this city.

I hunted in my bag for the card Eileen had given me, and then dialled the Hilton. Amazingly she was not in conference and her warm, capable voice was like a shoulder to lean on.

She told me what to do. 'Make a list of all the expenses you have had travelling here and staying overnight. Include your trunks here and back to Toronto, your fare back and add another hundred dollars for the inconvenience. Take the list and go to Mike Kirby with your luggage and don't leave till he pays you.'

I was overwhelmed. I would never have thought of all this.

'Then you come over here, and I'll see you off' added my kind friend. 'How are you for money right now?'

It worked like a charm. Mike Kirby paid most of it, with a wry look at this pushy English girl who knew the ropes so well.

After this I went to the Hilton where I had a real English pot of tea with Eileen. We got the trunks rerouted to Toronto, where I decided I would go, having burnt my boats in Brantford. Wild horses wouldn't have dragged me back to Mike at this stage. It was a matter of pride.

Why was I so different from other girls? To get married and settle down with a nice man and raise a family was all that many hoped for. Career minded young ladies were not much in evidence. A job in Chicago, as in Portslade, was only a stop-gap till Mr Right came along. Yet here I had a Mr Right waiting, and I was determined not to go to him. Call it pride, stubbornness . . . something I couldn't name drove me on.

Eileen agreed, reluctantly, to walk with me to the train station, which was about a mile away, as I wanted to get some fresh air, before getting on the stuffy, hermetically-sealed train. The streets were dark, their lights reflected in the puddles. We walked quickly, I carrying the little case which held my overnight needs. As we turned into one street I noticed out of the corner of my eye dark shapes lurking in shop doorways.

'Eileen,' I quavered, 'Do you see those men in the doorways?'

She didn't answer, but quickened her step and almost dragged me by the arm to hurry me along.

The next minute the world exploded. Guns blazed, whistles shrieked and men in trilbies and long overcoats sprung out of doorways, and from cars. Blaring sirens and the roaring engines of motor-bikes shattered my nerve as the street became the centre of a drama. It was just like a gangster movie and I was sure I had been somehow drafted as an extra.

Aiming at the sky I shouted, 'Is this a movie?'

'No sister,' came the swift reply, 'This is for real and you'd better get out fast.'

We scuttled away from the scene and just before we turned the corner I cast a quick look back and saw two men with arms in the air being marched to a big blue van.

4: Thin Ice

On the train I found my home for the two-day journey was a couchette. It was furnished with a couch which could be made into a bed, a shower, curtained windows and a door which locked to my satisfaction. I sat down and considered immediate problems.

The most obvious one was money. I had only twenty dollars left from what Mike Kirby had given me, after sending back fifty dollars to Dad, and returning my trunks, plus cost of the couchette. The next problem was what to do in Toronto. Contact Michael? No, that chapter was finished.

Then there was my luggage. I reckoned I was passing it en route as it went by slow train to Chicago.

Sitting with the door open, chin on hands, I happened to glance across the corridor and saw another traveller also sunk in thought, chin on hands. He looked so sad my gaze kept returning to him. As if conscious of my stare he looked up, our eyes met, and I said the first thing that came into my head to cover my embarrassment, 'Cheer up. Things must get better.'

He gave me a weary smile. 'If that's so, young lady, perhaps you'll tell me why you were looking as if you'd got the world on your shoulders, just now?'

'If you want to know, I was just wondering where my next meal is coming from.'

He sat up straight. 'I think we could solve that. If you would have dinner with me, you would be doing me a favour too.'

I accepted, thankfully, and we went along to the dining

car, and soon were settled comfortably at a snowy cloth, enjoying a sociable meal.

He seemed fascinated by the story of my adventures.

'You've got some grit honey. But I think you should come with me to Montreal. I can help you get a job.'

Seeing my expression he added quickly, 'Don't worry. It's all on the level. I'm still in love with my wife even though I've divorced her today.'

Al was a food scientist, married for fifteen years, with no children. His wife had walked out on him and gone to live in the USA with someone new. He badly needed a friend to talk to. As I listened I got the picture. He had neglected his wife for his work, and she had become bored and unhappy – with no family to care for. I told him this, out of the vast experience of my twenty years. He looked thoughtfully at me and said, 'You could be right. But it's too late now.'

Al was great company, during what could have been a tedious journey. He insisted on paying for my meals, and when I protested he overruled me.

'You've helped me, Ann . . . I can face going home now.'

But I refused to go on to Montreal with him. He was genuinely anxious about me and argued a bit, till in the end he said, 'I can see you're very determined to stand on your own two feet. Here's my number in Montreal. If you need me, call and I'll come.'

And he went, leaving me in the brightly lit station hall with not a friendly face among the crowds that jostled me. For a moment I was very tempted to rush after him, but almost immediately it came to mind that I had the number of Dave Draper, a Canadian I had known in England. He now lived in Toronto, and I had been unable to contact him during my previous stay. I phoned him at his Toronto office, and he told me to get a cab to his apartment. He would be there at eight o'clock. That meant there would be three hours to kill.

Another name popped suddenly to mind – Joan, my old

art teacher at Mile Oak, Portslade, married to a newspaper editor, was living in Toronto. I traced her number and immediately received an invitation to dinner at her house on an island in the bay. Joan at forty-five had just had a baby boy. She and her husband were kind and seemed concerned that I should not be on the streets, but were wrapped up in their new experience and I felt did not really want me to stay with them, so I did not impose myself.

'Dave Draper, here I come,' I said to the cold night air as the boat cut through the ice of the bay, back to the mainland. Thick flakes of snow were falling, and I shivered in my English wool coat which lacked the Canadian-style insulated lining.

Dave was the same pleasant guy I had known at home. We chatted amiably about mutual friends and about my experiences since arriving in Canada. Not till bedtime did I think about the geography of the flat. There was, it turned out, only one bedroom in which there was one double bed. A nasty suspicion rapidly turned into a certainty, and I had, painfully, to make the situation crystal clear to Dave. With bad grace he took himself off to the sofa in the living room. I said a quick prayer – a habit I had formed in childhood and kept up because it gave me a secure feeling – and slept like a baby.

Surely there must have been some guardian angel working overtime on me for I was certainly leading a charmed life. There seemed to be deep and dangerous currents in every situation I met, with a very thin covering of ice on top. As I stood on the shores of Lake Ontario and watched the speed skaters, with their bright bobble hats and flying scarves, skimming the ice, I saw myself as a lonely skater cutting figures across the new, smooth surface, aware of its treachery and my own vulnerability.

Monday morning I found myself a job at the Canadian Legion, at a salary of forty-five dollars a week. Through the *Toronto Times* I located a flat, sharing with two other girls.

Just before Christmas, however, I transferred to a rooming house, run by an English couple, in St Clair, Toronto. They looked after me, as I had got rather run down, through not having enough money to live on. At that time I was made redundant and had to find another job, which I did at A. E. Ames, one of the largest stock exchanges in Canada. I became secretary to the vice-president of the Municipal Bond Department. I got the job by cheek.

The agency sent me there, knowing I could do only 60 w.p.m. of shorthand, and that I had never used an electric typewriter. The job called for 120 w.p.m. The personnel manager gave me a test for both shorthand and typing and discovered that though my typing was good my shorthand was rusty.

'I'm sorry,' she said, 'You won't do, because we need 120 w.p.m.'

'Can't I see him, now I'm here? I'm sure that with practice, it'll improve.'

Call it luck, or cheek or both, but I got in to see the great man. He was old, at least seventy, and he gave me the impression that he shrank from super-efficient secretaries.

'Let me tell you a secret, my dear,' he said. 'I hate dictating. I always write my letters out myself.'

'I want to tell you a secret,' I said, 'I hate shorthand!'

'Good!' he said with a twinkle in his eye. And I had the job. That personnel manager's jaw dropped a yard and a half.

Christmas I spent with my mother's pen-pal Muriel. Her brother had sent the white skating boots, which mother sold to start me on my career. She was married with three children, and they were all Canadian-Lebanese. Here I sampled a real cross-cultural cuisine. Green jelly with grated carrot and peas in. Ham iced with glacé icing (yes, really!), thirty different salads at Christmas dinner and sweet rolls, peanut butter and molasses, when you least expected them.

35

In February, I was twenty-one and Mary, a friend I had made at the Canadian Legion, gave me a surprise birthday party for everyone I knew in Toronto: about sixty people. Michael didn't come, but sent me a bouquet of flowers.

I had been in Toronto four eventful months when I remembered why I had come. At the time I was looking down a list of towns and cities wanting investment for projects when I suddenly knew I wanted to move on. My feet were itching for travel. At once I got in touch with Gerald Palmer in England, for a promised introduction to Morris Chalfen of Holiday on Ice.

Gerald moved like lightning and in two weeks I had a contract in my hand from Morris Chalfen to join the company in Chicago and travel with them to Sioux City, Iowa. I gave my notice in to my kindly vice-president.

My sadly-battered trunks had to be replaced, and I needed rehearsal clothes. Rudi, who owned an illegal gambling casino had been taking a kindly interest in me, and he supplied me with these at no cost to myself. Help always came when I needed it.

Four friends from the Brighton Tigeresses Ice Hockey Club, Judy, Anne, Marianne and Mary, who had joined me in Toronto, remarked on my ability to find willing helpers.

'Ann, why is it you just have to look at someone and they jump to see what they can do for you?'

'I guess it's just a question of luck,' I replied, with a toss of my curly head.

I think too I had a very positive attitude to life. Events seemed to hum when I was around. That time when I had the judo accident at 17 was a case in point. I was thrown by a wrestler in the judo class, and I had an injury to my spine and legs, which took several months to put right. Going back on the ice I was afraid to do any tricks, so Dad and I cooked up the idea of an ice hockey club. A report of this in the *Evening Argus* produced fifty girls that same day, all eager to join.

Now my four friends, the backbone of the Tigeresses

were with me, and the club had disbanded. Together we went to watch a few ice hockey matches. I thought the Brighton Tigeresses were something special, but Canadian hockey moved like light. My four friends wanted to join a ladies' club but couldn't find one. It was strictly a man's dangerous game. When we went on the lake and started flipping the puck around the youngsters eyes popped.

In June however my trunks were packed and I was ready to go. At the train station once more, I saw my trunks into the guard's van with a quick prayer that we wouldn't part company this time. Judy, Anne, Marianne and Mary stamped out 'Good Luck' on a metal disc and gave it to me. 'Keep in touch so we can come and see you', they cried as the train pulled out.

At the border between Canada and the USA immigration officers found me in my compartment entertaining fellow passengers with stories of my travels. They gave me a work permit to enter the States. The ice looked good and smooth before me.

5: No Holiday

In the huge concourse of the Chicago train station the cast of 'Holiday on Ice' stood out for good looks. Casually dressed for the three day journey ahead they were at ease with themselves and with one another. I felt like a schoolgirl as I approached, though I hoped I was dressed to make an impression, with a smart black and white frock and carefully matched accessories. My thick brunette curls had been tamed into a sophisticated style. The members of the cast gave me a once-over, and then went on talking to each other as if I didn't exist.

My heart sank into my black patent shoes. If they were this unfriendly I could be in for a rough ride.

Morris Chalfen soon appeared on the scene, with the show manager, Ken Stevens. They carried boxes of sandwiches and drinks for the entire cast. This apparently was Morris's habit when we stopped anywhere. I looked my new boss over carefully. I did not want to get off on the wrong foot.

He was a small fat man, puffing on a big cigar. He stuck out a pudgy hand adorned with a gold and diamond ring, and there was another glint of gold in his wide smile.

'At last we meet, Terry,' he said. I was a little taken aback by this form of greeting, and told him my first name again. But he waved his cigar expansively. 'With all the Annes in this show . . . you're Terry!'

Morris called for someone by the name of Beryl to come and show me the ropes. She turned out to be a beautiful blonde from the north of England, who'd been skating with the cast for a number of years. I began to feel a little happier at being with 'Holiday on Ice'.

During the long journey to Sioux City, Beryl gave me the lowdown on my new life. She told me the tour would be very strenuous, with short stops. 'Sixteen cities in a year,' she said. This was not good news. It meant unending travel and maybe having to pay two hotel bills in one week. I thought wistfully of Skegness and Mrs Parker's digs. There were none like her here, evidently.

'They weigh us every week,' Beryl told me. 'We get fined two dollars for every pound we gain.' This was to keep to a minimum the letting out of seams in the expensive costumes, and to ensure that skaters kept their figures. Rehearsals started at 9am and went on sometimes till 11pm. 'And you only get half pay for rehearsals. If you can room up with someone you'll make out, otherwise you could find it hard to get by,' she continued.

By the time we got to Sioux City, I was glad to get off the train and out of that icy air conditioning which Americans like to maintain indoors. When I stepped into 100 degrees of heat it felt as if all the moisture was being sucked from my body.

Sioux City was a farming town. I remember the smell from its slaughterhouse. It stank when the wind blew in our direction! There I learned that England and America were two nations divided by the same language. 'Don't you find difficulty with our language?' asked one old lady in my hotel. I laughed but agreed I did.

'You call it the hood and we call it the bonnet, you call it the trunk and we call it the boot, you walk on the sidewalk and we walk on the pavement, we go up in a lift and you use an elevator, we cross the road and you cross the pavement,' I told her.

'And you have a b-a-r-t-h and we have a b-e-t-h,' laughed a gentleman standing by listening.

We were performing in the Civic Centre. The head seamstress had arranged the dressing rooms. The ice engineers had already made the ice. This was a complicated process. First they installed the generators and laid canvas and sand (to protect the flooring) then the pipes. Brine and other chemicals were pumped through, to create refrigeration. Then lorry loads of ready made crushed ice were brought in and shovelled over the frozen mass, and scraped and brushed to produce a glassy finish. All was ready by the time we arrived.

With Morris Chalfen's contract in my pocket I was startled to learn that I still had to audition, just like sixteen other dancers who had arrived from all over the USA. But I kept cool and used my head.

'Would you mind if I warmed up first?' I asked the choreographer. 'I've been roller skating all summer in Canada. The ice rinks are closed in the summer there.' He agreed and the seventeen of us who were auditioning went on the ice and whirled round. The size of the arena frightened me. It was Olympic size and bigger than anything I had skated on before. I ran through all my fancy footwork with a few jumps, spins, flying parallels and spirals. I suddenly felt free. My ice skates were so much lighter than the heavy roller skates I had been using. This gave me extra confidence and buoyancy. At any rate I made an impression on the choreographer. Over the mike he called out, 'All right Ann, you'll do. You needn't skate solo.' Was I relieved.

Backstage the seamstresses began measuring us and making costumes, which would be hung in huge metal wardrobe trunks. I shared one with Patsy Mar, a Canadian champion. She was sweet to me. We went around together and became good friends.

Rehearsal hours were long – as long and arduous as Beryl said they were – and we were on skates most of the time, with little chance of a seat. My feet weren't used to it and they swelled up. When we broke for lunch it took me nearly a half hour to walk to my hotel. No sooner had I arrived than I collapsed under the shower to soak my feet.

There was barely time to swallow a few mouthfuls of hamburger before beginning the walk back.

During the six weeks' rehearsals we were weighed in, and measured from the crown of the head to the ends of our big toes. We had to note the numbers we were in individually, and go for costume fittings for anything up to eight scenes.

On the ice the choreographer, Mr Hale, and his assistant, Annie Schmidt, would work out the markers, indicating where each person would stand. Lights would be placed around the square of ice, in blocks called 'headers'.

Meanwhile the lighting engineers would be placing the spotlights and beams to create spectacle, colour and atmosphere. The chief engineer travelled with us. Those who carried out his orders would be hired in the locality.

All this time the designers would be making sets, with the carpenters and painters. Stage-hands would be trained to handle the sets and the curtains and see that the props were to hand for the skaters.

I had never seen anything quite so elaborate as some of these sets. But this brought problems. In one Hawaiian number, Sherry had to manoeuvre a motorised float, while throwing blossoms to the audience. She didn't drive and was extremely nervous, became confused and lost control. The float went haywire, careering around the ice, carrying a screaming Sherry, before plunging into the headers. Sherry's Hawaiian skirt fell down. The audience roared with laughter, then, as the male skaters came to the rescue, extracting her from the float and escorting her off the ice, holding up the skirt as they went, cheering broke out.

We had an Indian number with totem poles and fancy steps, to Indian drum rhythms. There was one step I just could not master and we went over and over it. I didn't get it right till we got to Europe two years later!

Eight of us out of the 28-strong corps de ballet danced

'Swan Lake' on ice. This was not one of my favourite numbers. Again I was swathed in prickly white net, but this time they gave me a little discreet bust support. I had difficulty in kneeling on the ice. That old judo accident prevented me from bending my right knee. Mr Hale noticed this. 'Kneel Ann,' he called out, 'bend'. Down there on the ice my stiff kneee seized up. I ended with ice burn rings on my knees, imprinted with the fish-net pattern of my tights.

We had a world champion water skier in the cast. He had married a red-headed adagio ice dancer, Jinx Clark, and she had persuaded him to learn skating so that they could dance together. She was a wild character, an individualist, with flair, a fast rhythm skater, alluring, and a real pro of the old school. They don't make many like that today.

Alice, another soloist was a real lady. She dated Mr Stevens, the manager, and they eventually married. But I still found it difficult to break into some circles in the chorus, where the girls were unfriendly to me. A good proportion of the men appeared to be uninterested in girls, but they at least were friendly.

I gathered that some of the cast had been to Europe and had experienced resentment over their larger salaries, paid at the American rate, earned for doing the same steps as the poorly-paid Europeans. I determined that as new people came in I would make them welcome. So by the tour's half-way mark I had loads of friends, and didn't need to worry about American attitudes.

The first night was really splendid, with a champagne atmosphere of excitement. Getting ready was a nightmare, trying to remember the sequences and details of our costumes. I managed to remain calm, just full of anticipation. Rudi from Toronto, sent me a lovely pot of flowers, with a card. 'Good luck for the first night', it read. Other girls were surprised.

'You're not a star,' said two rather catty members of the chorus. I just laughed. 'One of our queer British customs.'

As we glided onto the ice, a long glittering line of girls and boys, drilled to perfection, we were met with wall-to-wall applause. Our costumes were spectacular – Victorian hooped skirts with bonnets and nodding feathers and huge muffs. We had a snowman, and a Santa Claus with reindeer and a motor drawn sleigh.

In one number we dressed up as toys and went out into the audience to greet the children. I was a doll with blonde hair and pigtails and eyes that blinked.

It was a really colourful show – a medley of Indians, toys, sailors, and Egyptian dancing girls. I found an advantage in being tall: I had the chance to do certain character parts with the principals.

Sometimes I had to pinch myself to realise I was not dreaming but skating in a top-class show, being paid to travel and see the world. My ambition had come true.

6: Second Sight

Publicity in the press spread the news in Sioux City that there were English girls in the cast of 'Holiday on Ice'. The good citizens loved to listen to a quaint English accent. I was invited out to a few places so they could hear it.

Girl Scouts made me welcome, and there I spoke about the show and answered some questions, inevitably about our Royal Family.

A little bright-eyed, blonde girl asked, 'Have you seen the Queen?' I told her I was in the Girl Guides guard of honour at the Royal Pavilion when she and Princess Margaret visited Brighton on one occasion.

'She stopped and talked to the girl next to me who had saved someone's life. So I had a good look. She was shorter than me even in high heels, and very well groomed, in a stunning blue outfit, with a matching hat. She was well made up, with pale complexion, and her eyes were really blue. . . .'

The girls hung on every word. I was a little less fluent on the subject of royal palaces and why the guards wore busbies.

We may have had the Royals to boast about but they had what I called civilization. Double glazing kept out draughts; homes and public buildings were air conditioned in summer and heated in winter; chicken, a luxury in England was a snack in fast food chains. Americans took their plenty as a matter of course.

One day a young man called Bob asked me out for a sedate milk shake at an ice cream parlour. I had never seen ice-cream in so many different flavours; even the names tasted good. I ran through a few varieties, like a school-kid.

'It's good to see someone enjoying themselves,' Bob commented with a laugh. 'Most girls I know are always talking about calories.'

Bob asked me next to his parent's home, for dinner. It was a revelation. At home we were still dazzled with the wonders of our first black and white TV, and my mum hadn't even an automatic washing machine. This American home was push button paradise, where every effort was reduced to the minimum.

Bob pressed a button in the car and the garage doors opened. We went into the kitchen, which had a gleaming array of push buttons and switches and levers, like the inside of a space ship. Bob's mother could open the back door, or close a window at the touch of a button. In their living room, Bob pressed a button and the whole wall slid back, revealing a bar.

'What would you like to drink, Ann?' I was asked.

'Orange juice, please.'

'And what in it?'

'I never drink spirits. I've got a sweet tooth.'

His family thought this real cute. When they had stopped laughing I said, 'What's so funny?'

'You are,' replied Bob. I couldn't see the joke.

The push buttons were sudden death to me till my reflexes caught up. I all but lost three cases and my right arm as the hotel lift doors snapped shut on me in Peoria, Illinois. Then, trying to find the button to open the doors again, I hit the one connected to the fire station, and called out the brigade. When we finally got on the train and were settled in our compartment, I hung my wardrobe case on the emergency cord, bringing the railway network to a halt. That was pretty good going for one day.

The ride from Grand Rapids, Michigan to Portland, Oregon through the Rocky Mountains was breathtaking in its splendour. The train hugged the curve of snow-topped mountains, burrowed through forests of redwood, sycamore, maple and fir, surrendered itself, shrieking, to smoky tunnels, climbing, ever climbing out of the valley up to the heights.

From the viewing platform at the back of the last carriage a great technicolour panorama of rugged country opened before me, in the middle of which I spotted a brown bear climbing a tree, and reindeer locking antlers. Above blue lakes and white waterfalls the sun lit a golden trail through thick forests ablaze with the fall.

Coming from a very densely populated country I was struck by the immense wild spaces and the comparatively few people visible in them. At one place an Indian encampment appeared, with tepees and open fires. A few hundred miles farther on a lumber camp sprang to view, with doll-sized men manhandling huge tree-trunks into convenient sizes for despatch down the mountain.

At night I climbed the stairs in the train to a glass-domed observation carriage. The stars sparkled like ice crystals just above my head, and the snowy mountain peaks glimmered in the strong, clear moonlight.

As I was going to bed on the first night of the journey I thought my eyes were playing tricks. Exquisite clusters of shimmering lights danced overhead, shifting and surging through the dark masses of trees, appearing and disappearing, as if some gigantic extravaganza were being staged for our benefit.

'What is it? Mary, Paul, what am I seeing?' I called out, rubbing my eyes. It was my introduction to the Northern Lights, one of the greatest shows on earth.

During the three day journey Lou, one of the show's comedians, asked me to manicure his nails. I happened to say casually, 'You've got a long life line.' His reaction was instantaneous. 'Do you read palms?' Unwisely, I played the question back. 'Of course.' I was in fact reading his palm right off my breakfast place mat, which had shown similarly placed lines with their meaning. Seeing he was impressed I ventured an even more rash prediction. I didn't know what made me say it, but I told him, 'You're coming into a fortune.'

He seized my arm in a steel grip. 'Ann, keep quiet about it. I want to carry on skating,' he hissed. It appeared that someone in his family had left him some money, and I had stumbled on his secret. At that stage, I was as surprised as he was.

From then on my name was Gypsy Rose, and I had a queue of customers. A lot of the fortunes I told were true or near enough truth. I told one chap he had been married three times. He turned white as a sheet because he hadn't told his current missus. Much of this was guess-work, but some of my 'hits' were regarded in a very superstitious way by others. Stage people believe fervently in luck, fate and mascots. Everybody needs something to believe in. I did too, and began to think that perhaps I had powers.

One thing I felt more and more was a need for something strong and stable at the centre of my own life. In the past, almost forgotten, was a whole lot of Sunday school and church attendance. We three Terry sisters went to St Nicholas Junior School, Portslade, and every Wednesday we marched solemnly to morning assembly in the church up the road. It put my cousin off God for years, but a sense of the sacred rubbed itself into my consciousness, to surface at moments of need. Packed in my case was a green Bible, which I took out sometimes and tried to read. But I didn't understand the terminology . . . all the 'begats' and strange instructions about sacrifices had nothing to do with real life.

The tour whisked us through every State of the Union barring Nevada, California and Alaska. We spent a week in each town or city, and it became very wearing to be always packing and unpacking, changing trains, waiting for hours at junctions, in badly heated stations, sleeping in cheap hotels and bolting down junk food in rushed hours between arrival and show time. It was go, go, go, with no respite. No wonder that tempers flared at times.

The show had its publicity manager, who went ahead and issued our pictures and details to the press. Out of a strong need to get away from the rest of the cast during free time, I had formed the habit of writing ahead to the Chamber of Commerce in each place we were to visit. When we arrived it meant I would be met and welcomed by someone, often taken out to dinner, or given hospitality. Certainly I never lacked for entertainment.

Knowing this habit of mine the publicity officer decided to play a little trick on me. Just before we got to Montgomery, Alabama, leaflets suddenly appeared on the train. I read 'ANN TERRY – GOD'S GIFT TO AMERICA. WE LOVE CHURCHILL. . . .' And the text went on about me and my ice skating. I was flabbergasted. Just what was going on?

As we pulled in I saw a huge banner stretched across the platform. It read 'WELCOME ANN TERRY TO MONTGOMERY'. A band played what I recognised foggily as Tommy Steele's hits. As I got off the train a man with a chain of office round his neck handed me a huge bouquet, and said 'Welcome to Alabama. We want to show you Southern hospitality.'

It gradually unfolded that the Chamber of Commerce had paid for my motel for two weeks, plus a car with chauffeur, so I could see the sights, and they were going to give me a farewell party on my last day.

As if that wasn't enough, they broadcast all about me on the radio and said '*This is Ann Terry's day. Show her Southern hospitality when she comes to your store. Give her a little taste of Montgomery to take back to England.*' I can hear it now. Every hour on the hour. It was just crazy.

I was showered with presents, and the press flocked around. I then knew who my friends really were in the cast, since most of the chorus girls were green with envy. The stars thought it was a laugh that I should be singled out for all this attention. I only realised later that the publicity manager had done it for a laugh – but the joke was on him.

In Birmingham, Alabama I suddenly felt lonely and homesick. It was Easter Sunday, and childhood habits reasserted themselves. I went to church. It was a real Southern Baptist service – and different from anything I had experienced at home. There were a lot of black people in church and the service went with a swing. As I went out the minister spoke to me, and remarked on my accent. So I told him I was with the show, and he introduced me to Jane, a college student with a most friendly smile. She promptly invited me to lunch. Her parents were sweet to me and we chatted like old friends about what I was doing and what Jane was doing at her college, called Stanmore, which turned out to be a Christian college. She was going to be a missionary. My idea of missionaries as old-fashioned plain folk like Sister Holland, the deaconess I knew in Portslade, did a somersault.

Jane invited me to one of her lectures at college. I made a date with her before rushing off to the show.

Two days later I filed in with all the other co-eds to a class in music at Stanmore. I was introduced to the music teacher, and he said a few words about me to the class.

After the session I had lunch with the dean of women, Mrs James-Sizemore, and asked her what were the possibilities of study at the college. 'I want to stay in America, but not carry on with show skating,' I told her. I had to think about the future as the tour was coming to an end in a month's time, and with it my work permit.

'I'll help, but we need a breakdown of your educational background,' said the dean on parting.

I set wheels in motion to get the information, and heard from her that there was every possibility of a physical education scholarship. I was elated for here was the green card, my gold key to a future in the USA. I had decided that life in show business was empty, and I wanted to do something more constructive with my life, perhaps make more of a contribution to society.

Jaded by living in such a highly artificial, and emotionally charged atmosphere all the time, cut off from normal contacts with the everyday world, I felt I was getting a distorted view of life. Frankly I and my fellow-skaters were growing tired of each other. Our attitudes were different, and they took the mickey all the time.

Getting off the train in the early morning to snatch a breakfast between changes I was bright and breezy; they all had hangovers and couldn't stand my chirpy manner.

At a party my colleagues tried to bring me down to their level, by putting vodka in my orange juice, but I detected it and gave it to the plants. From the other skaters' point of view I must have been Goody Two Shoes, an innocent abroad. It hardly endeared me to them. Even the reference I got from the manager mentioned my high moral character . . . it was the way I had been brought up.

My thoughts turned homewards, longingly. Suddenly, Portslade didn't seem quite so boring. I'd have given a week's salary for a quick glimpse of the gasworks.

In one city I went on the air to be interviewed, filling up a hole in someone's loose programming, talking about myself and the adjustments I had made in order to survive in the USA. The programme lasted an hour and unknown to me some of the cast were listening. I was surprised when about half a dozen of them came and apologised to me.

'We didn't realise how difficult it's been for you,' they told me. 'Don't let it put you off America.'

After that things were a little easier, but I still sometimes cut loose from the rest of the cast, and found new people to meet. That way I gained many new friends and when we returned to a place, perhaps years later, I would have somewhere to stay that wasn't a dreary, expensive hotel.

When we got to Mexico a strange thing happened. The cast was told 'We'll be here a month' so we bought leather goods and tripped around sight-seeing. I had a beautiful leather coat made, in a small factory. Then we were suddenly told we would be leaving in a few days' time. It was something political, involving finance.

One night in the dressing room I had a strong premonition that something was wrong with the aircraft we were to take in a week's time. So real was this that I spoke it aloud:

'Well I won't be going by that plane.'

The other girls turned to me. 'What do you mean?'

'I'll go by train or bus. I'll even walk it. But I will not be going on that plane. Something is wrong with it.'

The next thing I knew Mr Stevens, the manager, sent for me. 'What do you think you're doing, scaring the cast like this?' he demanded, frowning fiercely at me.

I stood my ground. 'I suggest you get in touch with the aircraft company. You'll find there's something wrong,' I insisted. 'We won't be leaving on that day. You can save the company a lot of money by extending the show.'

Finally my sincere belief got through to him and the following day he checked. After all, our boss Morris Chalfen had lost his whole family in a plane crash.

No one said anything to me but a notice appeared on the board announcing we would be staying over three more days. My reward came when we boarded the plane and I was shown to a first-class seat with the stars, instead of being in tourist with the chorus.

As I drank champagne and ate a first-class meal I mentally lifted my glass to Mr Stevens.

7: Rich Living

We arrived in Miami Beach , for our last stop of the tour, broke, with no show, and therefore no pay. I had exactly five dollars. The company had recommended the Princess Hotel, on the Sunset Boulevard. It was three star and only just within my means. Marie checked in with me but flew straight off to Tampa, Florida leaving me to my own devices.

I went to have breakfast in a restaurant, with Ginny, Johnny and Marianne. It was a lovely meal, with egg and bacon and toast and jam and cups of tea – but it cost me three dollars, a little over £1. 'You're sunk,' said a nasty little whining voice in my ear. The others went back to the hotel but I decided to explore this millionaires' playground. The irony of it hit home. Here I was in the most luxurious place on earth – and I hadn't a bean with which to buy my next meal.

I had my bikini with me, however, so I headed for the swimming pool of a splendid hotel. There were some sun-bronzed lifeguards in attendance, and it should have been an easy matter to get on speaking terms – but with the tanned blondes I saw cavorting around there was a sight too much competition. I beat a retreat. The next hotel was like a Hollywood film set, with its sweeping stairway and crystal chandeliers, and with a beautiful garden right in the foyer, set with exotic trees, and fountains gushing into pools in which goldfish swam.

All day I meandered along the Sunset Boulevard, cooling off now and then in the hotel pools or in the sea, while I studied the leisure habits of the really rich. Women of uncertain age floated on blow-up mattresses in hotel pools, coated in sun creams and Polyfilla make-up, wearing wigs and false eye-lashes, and loaded with jewels from their safe deposits. They glared at me, bobbing up and down on the water as I splashed past them, doing the backstroke. Probably they were decked out like that, I thought, because they were fishing for a third or fourth husband.

There were plenty of water faucets spouting ice-cold liquid. But by late afternoon I was very hungry. I reached the Hotel Plaza, haunt of the film stars and looked curiously up at its towering facade, wondering which window belonged to Frank Sinatra. I hoped to meet him on Friday when, like Cinderella I would go there to a ball, with the rest of the cast.

It was getting towards dusk and I was tired. I was walking slowly back up the Sunset Boulevard when out of the corner of my eye I saw a car tailing me. There were people around so I kept going. Then a voice hailed me, 'Hey, you have the most miserable face on the Strip!'

The voice belonged to a handsome tanned face and a pair of blue eyes.

'Thanks a lot. If you were in my shoes you'd look like this too.'

'You're English!' And with that blue-eyes stopped that car and got out to introduce himself. He was John Conway, an actor, appearing on Broadway. He invited me for a drink in a nearby club bar, and we talked about the show and I told him some of my adventures. He thought it was hilarious.

After a while he discovered I had no money. His eyes opened wider. 'I've never heard anything like this before in Miami. Look, you must be hungry. Let's eat. Waiter. . .'

Soon I was tucking into the most fantastic, fresh lobster. I had never had such a meal before – and with a famous star too!

He drove me back to my hotel and I had a shock when

the reception desk denied all knowledge of me. Suddenly John twigged the reason. My hotel was next door. The architecture was the same. Laughing, he asked for my phone number and invited me to a party on his yacht the following night. My prayers that night included a heartfelt thank-you to the guardian angel who had seen me through yet again.

The next morning I went down early, so as to have the swimming pool to myself before the diamond-encrusted hordes arrived, when I spotted a huge heated trolley bearing the sign 'Meals on Wheels'. From reception, I learned it was a room service for those guests who could not get out easily. Here was a way out of my financial difficulty. Back in my room I ordered meals on wheels for the rest of the week. Breakfast, lunch and dinner for five days came to $39, which I could pay at the end of the week.

After a breakfast fit for a queen, I went window-shopping for presents to take back, and then on to the ice rink to pick up my mail. There was an envelope in Mike's familiar handwriting. I shed a tear over the news it contained. He was married – to an English girl.

Stanmore College had sent me an invitation to sit an exam to assess my grades for scholarship entrance. That shut that door. I was in no mood to sit an exam and had no confidence I would pass.

The good news was a tax refund – enough to pay for a boat fare back to England. This made up my mind for me. I would go home. I had been away two years . . . it was too long. I went straight down town and found a travel agency.

At two o'clock I took a boat trip which wound around the bay, letting the passengers peek at the luxury mansions of the millionaires. Green lawns swept down almost to the water's edge.

'How do they keep them that way?' I asked one holiday couple. The man, gay in Hawaiian shirt and bermudas pointed out the sprinklers, which sent a fortune in fresh water cascading on the moist velvet. 'It takes dough, honey. Round here they spend it like water. . .' and his three chins shook with laughter at his own joke.

John Conway arrived at seven thirty pm to take me to dinner on his yacht. He wore a nice white jacket and a crisp shirt with a blue cravat, which set off to perfection that special Florida tan. As we crossed the carpeted foyer to leave the hotel, out of the corner of my eye, I saw some of my friends coming out of the lift. 'Just checking' I thought. I'd have done the same. We were all interested in each other's dates.

'Have a nice time, Ann!' I waved back to Ginny, conscious that I must have looked good to her critical eyes, in my slinky red dress and silver shoes and bag. John had a long, low Thunderbird parked outside, and we purred along the sea road to the marina.

'Oh . . . how pretty,' I exclaimed, when he pointed out his yacht. The outline of the rigging and mast were picked out in coloured lights, and music drifted over the water. Glittering couples sat on deck enjoying the night breeze, while white-coated waiters slipped between them balancing trays of drink.

It didn't take me long to work out that some of the girls were trying to catch the eyes of the affluent film producers on board. All the talk was of current Broadway shows and films. Some auditions were arranged right under my nose, there by the bar. To get ahead in this world, obviously you had to be at the right party.

Going home, at two o'clock in the morning, John said, 'You're very quiet. Did you have a nice time?'

'I certainly did. Your friends are interesting . . . but my world is so different.'

It wasn't only that my world was different . . . it was me that was out of tune. I thought of the good times, when the show was going well, and I had a good part, and my social life was fizzing. But this feeling of missing out on something solid and real waited in the corners of every hotel room, ready to creep out and confront me when I was alone and had time to think.

What was it I missed? Love? . . . A home of my own? In the spring I often felt a pang when I saw couples walking together in the park, holding hands. It was difficult to have someone permanent in your life when we were so constantly on the move.

But there was something else . . . an old pain . . . an ache felt when clouds were massing in the blue skies over the Rocky Mountains, or when I felt the mighty lift of the sea as I splashed at its edges, or watched the humming birds hover in the bougainvillaeas, or studied the perfect waxy curves of an orchid.

Next day, still thoughtful, I took myself off to the park for a morning stroll. And there I came upon an interesting sight. A group of children, about five-years-old I guess, sat, stood or knelt round an elderly lady who was sitting on a park bench.

She was very well made-up and wearing a soft, flowery dress that made her look youthful and well cared for. But what struck me was the big, black book from which she was reading. It was a Bible – and that relaxed and pretty group of children were riveted to it, judging by the looks on their faces. I sat down on the grass nearby, to hear what she was reading. The years dropped away from me and I was back in Mile Oak, listening to Sister Holland.

After a while the lady stopped and told the children to go and play. Then she turned to me: 'Well praise the Lord, when you can get the children in the park to come and pay attention to the reading of the word of God!'

I thought she must be a little eccentric, but obviously she loved children. 'Do you do this every day?' I asked.

'Every day. Children nowadays don't get so much about the Bible as when I was at school. So I just come along and tell them about Jesus. They seem to like it all right – and they even bring their friends!'

Before I left the park I received an invitation to visit her home for coffee later in the day. 'I'll have someone pick you up from your hotel,' my new friend promised.

So I went to coffee in a charming bungalow on the

outskirts of Miami. The garden had palm trees and the roof had solar heating panels which miraculously produced boiling water in the taps.

Miriam, my new friend, asked me if I had found a church yet in Miami. When I looked confused – church was never absolute top of my priorities – she invited me to go with her on Sunday. But before that there was, apparently, a Bible study to attend. 'Okay!' I agreed, ever ready for new experiences. It was one way to meet her friends, and who knew what might follow.

By the following Tuesday I had put in quite a few hours of church-going and was feeling rather unlike my frivolous self. Even my show friends started to comment on my thoughtfulness. Not bothering to go too deeply into what I had been doing I told them, 'I'm wondering what the future holds, in England.'

'What, aren't you coming back Ann? The new show is going to Acapulco and also to Canada. . .! Up to then other ice shows had had the monopoly on Canada so the cast were quite excited.

Morris Chalfen was really surprised when I turned down his offer of a contract for the next tour.

'What's eating you, Ann? Nobody turns me down!' And he puffed great gusts of cigar smoke over me, making me cough.

'I'm tired of living out of a trunk – two days here and three there. I'd like to study and learn something.' I told him about the offer of a college place.

He chewed on his cigar thoughtfully. 'Hmmm. Well, keep in touch. And if you ever change your mind get in touch with me. And come and visit me in New York on the way home.'

When I went to the Bible study the following Tuesday, the pastor of the church invited me to lunch. As we walked through the church on the way to his house, which was attached, I told him how alone I felt, and different from the other skaters.

'I don't have much in common with them . . . don't

57

drink, smoke, swear or stay in bed all day. I like to be out and looking at life,' I told him. He nodded understandingly, and then added something strange.

'You needn't be alone Ann. Have you ever asked the Lord Jesus Christ into your life?'

'What?' I asked, not understanding this at all. 'How do you do that?'

'Kneel down here with me and repeat this prayer after me.'

I did as he said, feeling he knew God as I didn't. I had been confirmed. Perhaps this was the next step to get to know God. I wanted to know him, as the people in this church seemed to.

The stone floor was cold. Outside the temperature could bake bread, but inside the air conditioning refrigerated us. I began to shiver, and hoped he would be quick about his prayer. But I dutifully repeated the words after him, not quite knowing what it was all about, or how it could work. I was destined to remain puzzled for a long time, but then God knows our hearts, and moves in on us when we are ready to receive what he has to give.

The pastor was over the moon. He rushed me through the church and into his kitchen, where he kissed his wife and said, 'Guess what Ann's done, honey?'

She turned with a smile. 'What has she done?'

They both looked at me and I looked doubtfully back.

'We talked . . . we prayed. . . .' What else? I couldn't think what it was I was supposed to say. The pastor's face fell, and he soon changed the subject. But a tinge of embarrassment remained, and I felt that in some obscure way I had let him down, and also missed out on a great secret.

8: Hot Ice

The last night of that memorable show, in Miami, on 2nd July, 1961, will always stand out in my memory. Morris Chalfen unexpectedly appeared on the ice, with a white-uniformed, gold-trimmed admiral, loaded down with medals.

The finale had been spectacular: a marine number, with the precision marching and rifle-twirling of the Queen Anne's Salute, ending with all 75 members of the cast flourishing flags of the nations of the world. Morris Chalfen made an important announcement – that the marine number had received recognition from the United States government, and we were to get an award.

We were delighted. Mr Chalfen and our choreographer, Mr Hale, received a magnificent shield and a parchment document from the admiral. All the girls were given flowers. Five thousand people watching in the sports arena cheered wildly. It was an immense honour for an ice show, but in the entertainment business we were ambassadors for the United States.

Goodbyes were said without much fuss. Facing me was a two-day journey to New York and then about five days on the boat to Liverpool. I was certainly looking forward to seeing Mum and Dad and putting myself on ice for a while.

* * *

Liverpool in the rain was not a pretty sight. Dirty, soot-blackened buildings, rubbish blowing about in the streets, people looking pale even though it was summer . . . I had left colour, warmth and luxury behind me.

As I got off the train in Euston a voice hailed me. It was Arthur, our friend and lodger.

'What's this about you giving up show business?' he demanded as we settled ourselves and the luggage in a taxi. 'You've got five telegrams waiting for you from that skating place in Germany!'

My eyes opened wide. The Casa Carioca Club in Garmisch-Partenkirchen, Bavaria, turned out the best. Anyone who was anything in the skating world longed to go to this famous school. Knowing this, in one of my fed-up moods during the tour I had written to Terry Rudoff, the Hungarian choreographer in charge of the show at the Casa Carioca to see if there was a possible vacancy. I had mentioned I was interested in comedy. Ice shows always seemed to be short on comedy. Having done that I had put the whole thing from my mind. What would be, would be. But now this letter had borne fruit. 'What did the telegrams say?' I asked, trying to keep my excitement from showing too much.

'Someone called Terry Rudoff wants you immediately, by the sound of it. She says they have a vacancy. You're to phone her at once.'

Immediately I jettisoned plans for leaving show business. To be wanted by such a choreographer and agent for so many ice shows was fantastic news. Thanks to experience with 'Holiday on Ice' I had become a good chorus skater and now perhaps I would even become a star. For the rest of the journey home my answers to Arthur were a little haphazard as my mind kept returning to a rosy dream.

In a circle of rainbow lights beaming down on the ice I saw myself skating solo. My costume would be short and lightweight, not flapping round my legs, like so many of the heavy costumes I had worn in the chorus line. A silver figure I spun and jumped, did flying parallels, sit spins, back edge spins. In the darkness outside that magic circle of light people applauded. We can all dream. My dream was to be a star.

Father met us at Brighton station with the van. He was so happy to see me. He looked at my huge hanging trunk and three suitcases with a grin, 'You've brought back half of America with you, haven't you?'

Mother, typically, was in the kitchen cooking up a meal, so I had to leave those telegrams alone till I had bolted it.

Terry Rudoff, when I finally got through to her, was brisk. 'Ann, when can you come?' she asked in her thick Hungarian accent, overlaid with American.

I asked for a week, pleading tiredness.

'But I want you quick, now please!' she said.

After a little persuasion on my part she allowed me a week. It was, however, two weeks before I showed up in Garmisch-Partenkirchen, and I felt pretty ragged, having travelled by train for thirty-six hours across Europe, with no real sleep. At Garmisch station at eight o'clock in the morning I was surprised to see waiting for me, Gillian Bainbridge, an old skating friend from Brighton days. I learned to my horror that I would have to audition right away for Terry Rudoff.

'She's waiting at the Casa Carioca for you. She wants to be sure that you can skate. I told her you can,' volunteered Gillian, looking at me sympathetically. 'You look shattered, Ann.'

I staggered on to the ice and did a few groggy spins, and some split jumps, a drag and a stag jump, finishing with my speciality – a right outside forward edge spiral, switching into a back inside edge, then twisting forward. I made sure to cover the whole rink, which was stamp-sized but cute, with balcony tiers of tables and chairs for wining and dining the patrons.

Suddenly there was a shout from the ice engineer, warning me to get off the ice. I saw to my amazement a wooden floor coming towards me over the ice. This was the dance floor, which they were about to clean and polish. That finished that audition, to my relief. Terry seemed pleased. But she looked me up and down quite carefully and then made a strange request: 'You need a nose job!'

It appeared that beauty was the aim. People had ears pinned back, heavy lobes trimmed, noses straightened, eyes rounded, sagging chins removed . . . all for the sake of stardom. Terry mentioned my appearance several times. She even wanted me to wear wigs, since my own hair was so frizzy. In the end I stamped my foot and said 'NO!' I wanted to remain my own natural self. The others in the cast quietly applauded my stand. However, I did make one concession. I went to Rene, the local hairdresser for the Americans and had my hair restyled, tinted and the kinks taken out. I was a new girl. Even Terry was impressed. She got a photographer to take my picture and then said, 'And now for your teeth.' I burst out laughing. What next? . . . There was no satisfying her.

One difference with this show was that stars took chorus parts, when they were not doing their solos, so the standard was extremely high. It was fast moving and brilliantly choreographed. I loved every minute of it.

My wish to do comedy was encouraged by Terry Rudoff. She said, 'Find yourself a partner and work out a routine and when you're ready show it to me.' So I found Tony, one of the boys in the chorus, who also happened to be a professional hairdresser. One afternoon, when he was helping me with my unruly hair, he said, 'This is a good place to find yourself a partner and get an act together, isn't it?'

I studied my reflection carefully before replying, 'That's right, and I'm looking for a partner for a comedy routine.'

'Hey, let's do something about it, then!'

So we worked out a funny adagio dance routine, which we practised on our friends at parties to enthusiastic applause. Tony was so funny that I collapsed with laughter every time we danced the routine. Slowly, we got more polished.

We lived on the American army base, in an annexe, so

were not short of dates, even if they had to climb down the drain pipes to meet us after the show.

Our schedule was pretty heavy. Looking back at the diary I kept at this time I find I was up at seven o'clock getting ready for early practise. By eight o'clock I was down on the ice, warming up. By nine o'clock Terry would be making changes to the numbers for that night's performance. Then we would go through new routines for a movie which the army were having made. Then would come periods of other practise – soft shoe, exercises for poise, then ballet, acrobatics.

We had a rest for lunch. Most people lounged about after that or went to bed, since the show didn't begin till ten pm after the dinner and dance session. Always with a superabundance of nervous energy, I usually spent my afternoons with the latest date on the Zutszpitz, the highest mountain in the region, where we walked or climbed among beautiful scenery, afterwards treating ourselves to hot chocolate topped with cream, while we watched the summer skiing from a hotel lounge balcony.

For some reason the subject of church came up with Lauren, one of these dates. He said he went to services on the base. That stirred a chord in me somewhere. 'You know, I'd like to go to church,' I said, 'Only I don't want to go by myself.' In a trice it was arranged that Lauren would pick me up on Sunday and we would go together.

At the base chapel I was made very welcome by the chaplain. He looked down at me, with a warm smile, and my heart missed a beat at his grey, grey eyes. But then I saw the big, thick ring on his finger and cooled off immediately.

'I think you're my first ice skater,' he said.

I found myself saying, hesitantly, 'I've got a few questions I'd like to ask you when you've got time.' All the doubts and uncertainties which hadn't been settled in that Miami church were there, biding their time. There was something more about God that I didn't know. Some people had his number, and could speak to him. My line was disconnected.

The chaplain was free on Monday afternoon and invited me to coffee with himself and his wife. I kept the appointment on my own. Lauren was confined to base that day. But again came disappointment. To this smart couple, religion was a social round. I couldn't communicate with them.

Out of the blue we were given a week's holiday so that the army could refurbish the annexe. I didn't want to go back to England. Instead I contacted my pen pal Vreni Heinrich in Zurich, and received an invitation by return.

We had never met in the flesh, though we had been writing to one another for about ten years. As soon as I got off the train and we clapped eyes on each other we both burst out laughing, and she threw her arms round me. That week was a success from start to finish. Vreni had bright auburn curly hair and freckles. She was a bundle of laughs . . . and so was her dad, whose tremendous sense of humour overcame his lack of English. We ate cheese fondue and reindeer meat, which was tasty and slightly sweet. We went sightseeing, and I saw my first can-can in a Zurich night club.

When I got back to Garmisch, Horst, the cocktail head waiter, my main boy friend, was at the station to meet me, with some sad news.

'My liebling, Tony, your partner, has cabled to say he is not coming back from England.'

I was very disappointed. Our much-practised comedy routine had gone down the tubes. With a pang, I realised that I was not going to achieve anything permanent out of this period. It had been a marvellous experience, but I had to look to the future, and make another move to avoid a rut.

It was then that Gerald Palmer, my old boss, came to mind. I wrote to him in London at Great Windmill Street, near Shaftesbury Avenue. Back came a contract to appear in a principal understudy role, in the 'Wizard of Oz on Ice' at Wembley, starting in November.

Almost the last thing that happened in that period was the movie-making. Cameras rolled in and producers went round taking light readings, talking gibberish words like 'zoom', and 'pan', and handing out cues to the cameras so they could pick up where we were in the fast-moving show.

'Get in quick there! Too slow, you've missed that jump! Now you've cut off their feet! Terry, can you get them to do that part again? Ready?' I found it all very boring.

Packing to go home I thought over what I had learned in six months: to be more professional, better groomed, more versatile. . . . That was for sure. Also I could do solo numbers, which certainly wasn't possible before. Terry had put my act together, helped me to select music, and polished me. This skating finishing school would be my passport to an exciting future. Of that I felt certain.

9: With The Wiz

Because of the movie-making I arrived a week late for rehearsals at Wembley stadium – a draughty barn of a place. I reported at once to Gerald Palmer.

He had bad news for me. 'I'm sorry to disappoint you, Ann, but the choreographer has had to allot the principal understudy role to someone else. You'll be an understudy, but get your contract salary.'

I didn't care about the salary – I wanted the opportunity. Sometimes on three-show days the understudies got the chance to stand-in for a star. It was a blow to my hopes.

Seeing my downcast expression Gerald Palmer went on: 'You'll only have six numbers to do, so learn as many parts as possible. You never know what might happen on such a large surface.'

It was wonderful, zooming on to huge, Olympic-sized ice, after Garmisch. But the cast of 100 were of differing standards, and some were nowhere near the level of excellence I'd become used to with Terry Rudoff. On the other hand, the sets were brilliant.

In one scene Dorothy was sheltering in a barn. Then a tornado hit and the barn went up in the air and so did she. At that point the 100 piece orchestra crashed and banged with fine fervour, working up a storm of their own.

In my understudy role, I must have been one of the tallest Munchkins ever on the Yellow Brick Road. Patsy, who was pregnant, found her costume so hot and stuffy, so on a three-show day I stood in for her.

In spite of things not turning out as well as I had hoped I

loved being in the show. The atmosphere was so English and relaxing. We had Sundays off. We could sit in our costumes and eat and drink without being fined. There was a canteen available for snacks. One day when Chalfen came back behind the scenes and said 'What are you doing in a third-rate ice show, Terry?' I was able to say, 'Relaxing and staying put for a while.'

'Let me know when you want to come back to "Holiday on Ice". We're touring Europe and the Far East. If you want to get married Ann, the Far East's the place. I lose all my girls there.'

I grinned amiably: 'I'll think about it.'

One frightening incident occurred. A short circuit in power lines caused a fire in our dressing room. We were on the ice when smoke began to drift across the arena. The audience became restless. We stopped skating, but the orchestra ploughed on bravely. We were told to keep skating while the audience was shepherded to the side of the arena farthest from the fire. It was under control in ten minutes, but there was a major flood backstage, and the dressing room was gutted. Our costumes went and all our rehearsal clothes, our coats, shoes, spare skates, make-up. I mourned my carefully knitted sweaters.

'The show must go on,' said Gerald Palmer and obtained new costumes, but nothing was paid to the eight of us for out lost belongings. Still, we had a job and our lives were safe. The fire was so sudden and fierce there could have been a tragedy. I felt that God was watching over us.

I was in digs with a super couple called the Johnsons. I got their address from the Actor's Church Union, with whom I had had contact since Skegness days.

It was always hard to find digs in Wembley because a lot of the landladies didn't like show people, and there were few hotels. But from the time I walked into the Johnson's house I felt the lovely atmosphere about the home. Mrs Johnson told me she had never put up a show person before. I could tell she was a little uncertain as to how to treat me. On the wall of the yellow, sunny room was a picture of Christ on the cross, looking down at the world. She stood in the doorway and watched me. 'Do you like the room?' she asked. 'Yes,' I replied. 'It's very sunny. I would like to stay, if that's OK with you.'

So it was settled and we all hit it off very well. There was so much love and warmth in that house and they really cared for me, even to picking me up by car between shows to make sure I had three meals a day, to keep up my energy. And when I had to go into hospital to have all my wisdom teeth out they came to visit me. The Johnsons weren't ashamed of showing affection to each other. She would sit on her husband's knee, which was difficult as she was twice his size around, but he bore it very well. I adopted them as my second mum and dad.

On Sundays, when I didn't go home, they took me to the Anglican church. A young clergyman with fiery red hair preached a lively sermon, and I felt the friendly, caring interest of the congregation reach out to me. There was no pomp and ceremony about them, and what is more they could enjoy themselves in other ways than just churchgoing . . . badminton for instance, which I sometimes played in their hall.

The show was due to end on 8th March, and my contract with it. Gerald Palmer called me into his office in Great Windmill Street, 'Ann, this show has done so well, and is so popular that I've had requests from other cities to take it around. It's been a long time since an ice show has toured England, so I'm really excited. As you have put so much into the show I'd like to give you an opportunity to join us. I've selected you and seven other girls to tour with the show. What do you say?'

'Great. Thanks very much.' Expecting to be out of work I had been looking into film or stage work, modelling in the Far East . . . anything that promised to be stimulating and involve travel. I even interviewed to be an air hostess, but turned it down on the grounds that it was glorified waitressing.

68

Suddenly I was no longer tired of skating. Three months in one place had worked the cure. Sometimes, of course, it was a chore to have to learn endless routines, and stay up half the night rehearsing. But mostly it was good fun, like a holiday, and not like a proper job. I looked forward to seeing England properly for the first time. I'd travelled right across America and Canada, but I hadn't seen much of my own country.

It was touring all right, for eight months but I only did five, because in Liverpool Bill Bailey brought the European director, Skee Goodheart, to see the show. They came backstage and asked me to go to the Far East with 'Holiday on Ice'.

'You look good on the ice, Ann. I hear from Bill that you've been working with our company in America, and we've had favourable reports,' said Skee. He was a tall, distinguished-looking man, with an agreeable manner.

'Thanks,' I said, 'But I'm not really interested in staying two days here and four days there. . .'

Bill Bailey quickly cut in, 'Ann, you'll love it. They stay a month here and a month there so you can get all the rest you need.' In the end I heard myself arranging to go to an ice rink at Aldrincham, near Birmingham, where I could try out on a big stretch.

I passed the audition and Bill promised to send me a contract to start in September. Blithely, I went home to get ready for a hot-weather tour. But when the contract came I was alarmed to see it was for Europe. I got on the phone at once to Bill Bailey. 'I've had all these dresses made for the Far East,' I said with some heat.

He said soothingly, 'Don't worry Ann, people who go to the Far East get forgotten quickly. You need a couple of years in Europe first to get known.' There wasn't much I could say.

When the Wizard of Oz came to Brighton, I took Mother to see it. I could sit back and look at it with the critic's eye. I was pointing out the details to her when I noticed she was crying.

'What's the matter?' I asked.

'I've never seen you skate in a big show yet.'

'Cheer up, Mum, you can always come and visit me in Europe.' This, later, was what she did.

We were told that we might be touring for two years without a break. That meant renewing skates, replacing my much-abused trunk, and stocking up in make-up, as we couldn't rely on local supplies.

In August, armed with all the European language dictionaries I could find – French, German, Italian, Spanish, Dutch and Portuguese – I set off to join 'Holiday on Ice' at Nantes, Brittany.

This show had everything – polish, glamour, class, originality. We were skating on Olympic-sized ice, with real stars – 21 Olympic and national champions from different countries turned professional. We skated difficult, fast precision numbers. To make it even more exciting I knew some of it already.

Our Parisian designer had produced sensational costumes for the opening number. Four of us, acting as show-girls, wore black velvet, silver trimmed, giant hooped skirts. They were draped over scaffolding 12ft high and we climbed up the scaffolding, under the skirts, to get into them. Then, perched on our precarious towers, we were pushed around the ice by two chorus boys, secreted under the skirts. The effect was magnificent.

While we gyrated gracefully around to the tune of Moon River, solo star Liz Kaufman was lowered from the ceiling in a portrait frame. Stepping out of the frame the 'portrait' came alive and danced on the ice. We crinoline ladies glided off, climbed down from the pedestals and donned fur-trimmed transparent capes over our black velvet leotards. Meanwhile twenty-eight girls stepped out from behind huge fans, which had been lining the stairs, and they made a graceful chorus line, in which we showgirls joined.

My favourite number was Twenty Four Hours in the Life of a Man. Love, War and Peace were its themes, and it lasted for half an hour of fast, rhythmic action. I was given a part, and threw myself into being a slinky gangster's moll. The audience loved the whole number. We had a first-class orchestra, excellent sound and Ted Shuffle, the choreographer from New York, produced these new, vibrant and challenging numbers for us to learn. In short that show was totally professional . . . just about the best I have ever skated in.

When we were on the ice we had to think constantly about what we were doing. If we kicked back we might hit someone's shin bone and gash them with sharp blades. Anyone unfortunate enough to receive it could be off for two weeks on half pay, while the stitches healed. We had no union to protect us – we didn't come under Equity ruling in Europe. For my own peace of mind I took out special insurance to cover dentist and doctors' bills. I didn't forget that accident which had spoiled my chances at fourteen years.

Another problem with the show was remembering all the accessories – what went with what. Hats, cuffs, gloves, jewellery, wigs, tights, fancy pants all had to match up with changes of costume. Forgetting anything meant a fine. Two dollars for forgetting part of your costume, two dollars if you were late for a number, four dollars for being late for the show. There was a scale of fines for drinking, eating or sitting in costumes. And as I have mentioned before it was only half pay for rehearsals. In spite of all this we loved our job. I sometimes wondered why.

You had to think for other people too. Not everyone was at the same standard. I was one of the most experienced line skaters, but I encountered real difficulty in the four-spoke wheel where I, more than 5ft 9ins tall on skates, had to go under the arms of girls a good six inches shorter. More than once it resulted in my side-swiping someone's skates and knocking them off balance, like dominoes. Then the audience would be treated to the sight of sliding bottoms as the girls hit the deck.

Afterwards in the dressing room my name would be

mud in French or German. Dismayed I went to Ted Shuffle . He saw I was losing my confidence and asked me if I would like to be put on the end of the line. 'Go out there and show them, Ann' he said.

To be on the end of the wheel you had to move fast as the line turned on its own centre, but I was in my element, though it was hard work. After a bit I came in out of the cold and the squawkers were put on the end of the line to prove themselves. Disaster followed, usually, until Ted slowed down the music and rearranged the line and everyone shut up about Ann Terry.

One of the Palais des Sport's less attractive features was the number of tramps sleeping around the hot vents in the outer courtyard, each one keeping out the cold with his bottle of vino. One morning as we came in one tramp did not move aside as we stepped over him, to get into the building. Then Kim, one of the girls screamed, 'Look at the blood! He's been knifed!'

We took a horrified look at a large knife sticking out of his side. The gendarmerie were nonchalant: 'It happens all the time. They drink, they quarrel . . . they take the knife to each other . . .,' said one officer with a very Gallic 'what-else-is-new?' shrug.

It made me very sad that life could be so cheap. Surely human beings were meant for a better end than that?

In spite of all the hard work in the show we managed to have some fun. A few of us hired a car and we toured Brittany during the rehearsal period. The rugged coast reminded us of Cornwall, and in the villages women sat in their doorways, making lace.

Patsy became my room-mate. She had been in the show for years and knew all the angles. She watched out for me, made sure I saved, booked hotel rooms, shared food, advised me on rates of exchange and on the finer points of the languages we met.

In Lille the girls began to go down with flu. We were performing in a huge unheated exhibition hall, with eight doors opening straight out on to the icy street. Huge gas

72

burners brought in to defrost us made little impact on the refrigerated atmosphere. We wore fur coats for rehearsals and then had to throw them off to go on the ice in skimpy costumes.

Patsy and I spoke up for the rest of the girls.

'Can't we wear our vests?' we asked. The choreographer did a double take:

'VESTS? In Scheherezade?' His eyes bulged.

I pointed out that we were sitting about with bare midriffs and legs in an Egyptian palace, while he was dressed for Siberia in fur coat and Cossack hat backstage.

'The girls are going down like flies with flu!' I said. 'And then you've given us all these extra numbers. You've got to do something or you won't have a show.'

He saw the point. 'Right, flesh coloured tights and vests,' he conceded. I still went down with a cold in my liver and was off work for two weeks with no pay. But different people rallied round and brought in special food for me.

10: Accident!

We flew into West Berlin through the air corridor over East Germany, knowing that if we strayed or flew below a certain altitude we might be shot at. However, all was well.

The press greeted us at the airport. It was a big publicity event because 'Holiday on Ice', the best in Europe, had not been to Berlin for years. The German sponsor, Horst, a wealthy manufacturer, asked Patsy for an introduction to the girl in the red dress.

'That's Ann', said Patsy, pulling me along to meet him. I tried to brush her off – my mind elsewhere. 'I'm worried about my luggage' I groaned. 'It hasn't turned up.'

But the manufacturer had influence. Not only did he invite me to dinner, with Patsy and Sylvaine, but he also got the airport to trace my luggage, which, true to form, was still in Lausanne.

Horst took us to dinner and then dropped us off at the Rese Bar, which was full of American airmen who were undergoing a shortage of ladies. As a result of meeting so many people I was rarely without a date for the rest of the tour in France and Germany, whenever we were near enough to an air force base.

It would be easy to get the wrong idea here, but in those days there were discreet barriers, which could only be crossed if the girl permitted. 'Holiday on Ice' girls had to watch themselves. If our private life hurt the company image, then discipline followed – fines, suspension or sacking. So in public we were careful – and we had a lot of good, clean fun.

A very few of my dates obviously had the wrong idea because I was in show business. I soon put them straight about that, with a firm hand-shake at the end of the evening, to their immense surprise. They usually then booked up for another date to see if they had dreamed it.

Some of my friends decided to go into East Berlin by train the morning after we arrived. I went with them, through the checkpoints, into a fabulous main street empty of people and cars, so different from the prosperous hustle and bustle of the West. A man came up to us and spoke in English. There was something stealthy in his manner. 'Look behind the facade!' he gritted and turned quickly away.

What could he mean? Patsy drifted casually down a side street and signalled to Bill, Joan and myself to follow her. We were amazed to find that behind the main Strasse was a ruined city. Craters, tumbled buildings still remained from the bombing of wartime. People clambered over the ruins and looked at us blankly. They seemed afraid to approach, though they were curious. Patsy, who spoke excellent German, said something to an old lady, who answered her briefly and moved away. 'She says that this is how it is. They live like this and it is difficult to get food and other supplies. The stores are just for the tourists. They can't afford the prices.' It was an eye-opener.

We got back to find that we had been on afternoon television without knowing it. The programme was beamed from a cafe we had visited in the eastern sector. 'Look, see how the tourists are coming to our fair city' was the message. We had been unwittingly used as propaganda.

We moved on, to Dortmund and then with Christmas in the air, to Brussels, to skate at the Palais de Sports. The Grand Palaza was lit with golden light. I stood by the huge Norwegian pine tree, hung with ribboned packages, tinkling bells and jewelled baubles which caught the light from cafes and shop windows, and broke it into a myriad brilliant facets. Carols filled the air and I felt as if I were a

75

child again, filled with the wonder of Christmas. My nostrils twitched with the pungent scent of pine. As I walked through the cobbled streets, looking for the unique little gifts I always hoped to find, I felt money was no object. Like all show people I lived for the present.

In self-defence I bought my sister a wool dress – she always liked to borrow mine. My mother got a bed-jacket – while I was in Berlin she had had a car crash and she was in hospital. I bought Father an unusual alarm watch. I did not know how I was going to get the presents home, but that was solved for me when, at the Christmas party an announcement was made that owing to a fire in Ghent we would be able to have a week at home. Our next engagement was cancelled.

Yippee! A Christmas holiday without ice. That was okay by me.

1963 . . . a whole new, bright year opened in Frankfurt, launched with a party on a barge. From then until May we spun through one country after another, going north till in June we arrived in Scandinavia. Then we turned south, following a route to Italy.

In Paris we rehearsed a new show, so we were at the Palais d'Exposition for seven weeks. In that time I had eleven driving lessons and somehow got through a test with a Parisian examiner.

He spoke no English, apparently, but kept asking me 'Pourquoi?' and mopping his brow with a white handkerchief as we drove shakily through narrow streets in the morning rush hour. Was he asking himself 'Why me?' At any rate he passed me – and then produced a bottle of champagne and two glasses, like a conjuror. The occasion seemed to warrant it.

In Marseille I met a squadron leader on the aircraft carrier, Saratoga. I thought he was joking when he invited me to dinner, but I ended up eating at the captain's table in the second largest aircraft carrier in the world.

One of the acts in the show was badminton on ice. If you think that's impossible, I can tell you it moved so fast that

76

the eye could barely follow. Shirley-Marie, then an American badminton champion, had learned to skate and joined the Forgies. Hugh Forgie, eleven times world professional champion, and his son, Reg also a world champion had a very clever act. Shirley-Marie was the 'feed' returning every serve, and hardly letting anything past. We became good friends.

Shirley-Marie bought a new Cortina in Marseille. That led to an invitation to me to drive with her down to our next engagement in Rome. We had two and a half days to cover nearly 1,000 miles.

I was distinctly nervous as we hit the road to Rome. Italians drove with gay abandon, heads turned to look at the blonde signorinas. I was brassy blonde from a bottle at that time, and it certainly was fun. After about 500 miles I began to feel like an old hand at driving on the right – and at avoiding suicidal drivers in three-lane skirmishes.

At Rome we had three shows over a weekend and a few well-known actors and actresses came to see us. I went out with a film producer who took me to a night club, Club 83. And there I met the Beatles.

They walked in with a big crowd which was largely dressed in scruffy old clothes. The orchestra happened to be playing Beatle music at the time, really loud. Beatlemania was at its height. Personally, I wasn't that keen. Glancing at this crowd I remarked casually to my producer friend, 'Oh, they look like the Beatles gone wrong.'

He eyed me strangely, and yelled (to be heard over the music) 'What do you mean, honey? They are the Beatles . . . I've just signed them up.' With that he dragged me over to the group and called 'Paul, here's a limey who doesn't believe you are a Beatle.'

I found myself looking at a familiar pudding basin haircut, a schoolboy face and eyes which shone with amusement. He was the best dressed Beatle, in a real suit.

'Care to dance?' he drawled in that dead-pan Liverpudlian accent.

'Yes,' I replied, determined not to be overawed, 'But if you don't mind I'll do my own style.'

So he swayed on one spot while I wriggled on another. 'You're a good mover,' he commented drily. I asked him how he was getting on with the latest movie, not remembering its name. In bursts above the music I learned how difficult it was to switch from performing as pop stars to acting the parts, coming in on cue, following the action. He seemed pleasant, and unaffected by success, with an engaging ability to laugh at himself . . . to stay detached from the whole pop scene, and not be taken in by fame.

Next day, at the show there was pandemonium, when all the young skaters came running in to squeeze me dry about the Beatles.

'Lucky you . . . what was it like dancing with him?'

'It was nothing special. He's just an ordinary English chap.' What sacrilege!

We didn't get a full house in Rome, and were glad to move on to Turin. Again I travelled with Shirley-Marie, sharing the driving. The show was to be in the Palais des Sports, for two weeks.

Halfway through our stay there, Heinz, the ice engineer, and his wife Heidi, invited me out to celebrate his birthday, with Ilona, the Swiss secretary. Returning from the restaurant, one block exactly from the hotel, Heinz started to cross at a junction. Then, twenty yards away we saw small, dim lights which materialised suddenly into a gigantic transporter truck – and it was bearing down on us at full speed.

I tried to pull Ilona over to my side, but she didn't understand and resisted. In horror I watched the truck come on, frozen rigid as in one of those nightmares when you try to escape from some nameless terror – but stay rooted to the spot.

The truck smashed into the off-side, and crunched the metal, crushing Heinz and Ilona. In that split second

I cried, 'God, I am not going to die . . . it's too soon.'

A voice spoke to me quietly, 'You are going to live.'

The next moment my arm was lacerated with glass, and blood dripped on it from Ilona's head, which I was cradling in my arms. Heidi was nowhere to be seen. The door was open. Heinz was still sitting in the driving seat . . . his ribs crushed.

I heard sirens. Someone reached into the crumpled car and asked me my name. I couldn't remember. A helpless feeling possessed me.

They disentangled us from the car wreckage and got us to hospital. Ilona the worst injured, with a fractured skull, was on the danger list. Heinz was strapped up and put on prolonged rest. I had bashed my head against the side of the car, which accounted for the loss of memory, and was treated with an ice pack to the head. Heidi – found running hysterically along the road, calling for help – was given a sedative for shattered nerves.

Fiat paid our bills, also replacing damaged clothes. Mine were covered in blood, and my shoes and bag had been taken by thieves, while I was still in the car in a barely conscious state. In the end Fiat also settled for a silver bracelet stolen from me in the car, a broken watch and time lost from the show, plus compensation for the injury. Ilona's five month convalescence was paid for, and Heinz's new car.

During my two week stay in hospital Derek Boyle, the manager, came to see me and I asked him to telegraph my mother about the accident.

'I wouldn't do that,' he said. 'You don't want to worry her. You'll soon be all right.'

But I insisted. 'She'll know,' I told him. I knew this from previous experience. Sure enough, two days later came a telegram from Portslade: 'I feel you've had an accident, but you are all right now.'

Derek brought it to me and I read it to him. He looked astonished. 'Ann I never did phone her.'

There was a pause and then he said, 'So it's true what happened in Mexico, then?' I realised that someone had been talking to him about the plane incident.

When the show moved on to Napoli the specialist refused to release me, on the grounds that it would be too hot for me in the south of Italy. I was still suffering from terrible headaches. But a few days later Nina, an Italian girl I had met on the boat the year before came to see me.

'How did you know I was here?' I asked.

'I read about you in the newspaper,' she said, producing it. There I was, crowned with an ice pack. What a publicity picture! How the paper had got it, with the beady eyed nuns guarding me, I couldn't imagine.

Then I recalled one visitor who had opened his coat as if to take it off. There had been a brief flash of light – and the next minute he was hustled out by sisters. He must have sold the picture to the papers.

The specialist allowed me to go to Nina's vineyard home, with Fiat's chauffeur ensuring a comfortable journey. So I had a wonderful, restful two weeks in a beautiful home at Castello di Fell, in the mountains outside Asti.

Soon after this, in San Remo, the show closed. Most of the skaters were paid off, but I was selected, with some others to start a completely new show in Nice a month later.

11: Sweet Sorrow

Rehearsals for the new show took place in Nice, where the August temperature was over 90 degrees. When I had a Sunday free I went to church. It gave me comfort and some sense of continuity in my travelling life.

In the cool English church I found a plaque commemorating Henry Frances Lyte, who wrote *Abide With Me*. This was my grandmother's favourite hymn – she was always singing it, and wanted it sung at her funeral. It was this grandmother, Nanny Terry, who gave me my first Bible, when I was eight. It was my birthday request. Nanny and Poppa Terry were so thrilled that I had asked for it, but Nanny said quietly, 'Wouldn't you like another present as well?' I shook my head. That was all I wanted. The green cover made me think of emeralds, and a handful of those precious gems would have seemed no more of a treasure than my Bible.

They still went ahead and gave me a beautiful doll called Topsy which grandmother had dressed herself. She was a seamstress, making fashionable ladies' dresses, as well as coats for three growing granddaughters.

Nanny Terry made me my skating dresses – the first was a pretty blue crepe, with a high cummerbund. The last dress for an amateur competition was her handiwork too – a Scottish plaid.

In my mind's eye I carried a picture of that warm, loving woman as I remembered her, carrying plates of hot food up the hill to neighbours who were sick. Her door was always open to those in need. A great sadness overwhelmed me as I remembered the good times spent with her sitting and talking in the parlour by the old black range which she kept bright. She and grandpa were with God and were looking down on me now. I just knew it.

On the heels of these thoughts came the voice that spoke only in the quietness: 'What is life all about? Will you ever have anyone to care for you?'

Out in the streets love was in the air. Couples strolled along the promenade holding hands, children were being kissed and indulged by fond parents. Romantic music was played at the bandstand. But there was no one for me. Loneliness swept over me.

The moment passed, as it always did. Life was too full of things to be done. Trains to catch, hotels to find, rehearsals, shows, and after shows, supper parties, dances, and a round of pleasure to shut out the fact of loneliness. But I experienced that bitter pain over and over. It was not only that I didn't have a permanant partner like most of the girls . . . I felt different in every way to everyone else in that show.

I once enrolled for a correspondence course with a school of writing in London, with some idea of maximising my talents in another direction. All the time I strove for an identity. Who was I, after all?

Most people I knew in Portslade spent their lives rooted to one spot on the face of the earth. They had the same friends as they grew up, went to school, found a job and married. They knew who they were and where they came from. Not only had I cut myself off from my roots, but I had not achieved that supreme affirmation of identity: the finding of the 'other half ' . . . the one who would help me discover myself.

Show business was no help. In some ways the travelling, roving kind of life was interesting, even glamorous. But I knew all that went on backstage, and was weary of it and determined not to go that way myself.

I got on well with the 'gay' crowd. They talked to me about their affairs, and helped me with my luggage. They usually had a good sense of humour, having learned that laughter is a shield against outrageous fortune.

In a bar after a tiring sixteen hour rehearsal, Carl and I were taking the weight off our feet. I could see he was unhappy, and gently probed. It appeared that his special friend was going around with someone else, and he was feeling the keen bite of loneliness.

'How did this all start with you?', I said. 'I want to understand. Can you tell me? Surely people aren't born like this? How did it happen with you?'

He took a swallow from his cognac and he looked at me with big, mournful brown eyes. 'Do you really want to know?', he asked in his thick German accented English.

'Not if it's going to be too painful for you to say.'

But he was launched. 'You know, Ann, you have a charming way of getting things out of people,' and he patted my hand.

'My mother, she wanted a girl and I came along. She would dress me up, and give me dolls to play with, and all girls' toys. I always played with girls, never with boys till I went to school at six-years-old. Then I had to dress in knickerbockers . . . it was hard. I had to play with boys and boys' toys.'

He told me the most painful experience came when he was called up for the army. They tested his claim that he was homosexual, found it true, and dismissed him on the spot. But it left him shattered. Not to be accepted by society was devastating.

Then it was my turn to go under the microscope. 'And what about you, Ann? Are you a virgin, still, after all these years of travelling with ice shows?' I told him I was. 'Can it be true? Surely not,' said Carl, opening his eyes wide with astonishment. 'You seem a very loving kind of person.'

'I'm saving myself for Mr Right,' I replied. It was true. I may have been quite naive, but I guarded myself jealously, remaining above all the hanky-panky. There could, for a girl, be consequences. I did not want to have to leave the show through someone else's selfishness. At that point other people came in and the conversation ended. But it went on working in my mind over the next weeks.

In Paris, I was staying at a family hotel near the Marie d'Issy subway, not far from the Palais d'Exposition, where we skated. I had no room-mate. She had gone off to live with her boyfriend. This was a disappointment to me. To be alone in Paris is no fun. I looked for a substitute.

In due course I met Harry, a singer at the Lido, whom I had known in the 'Dick Whittington' pantomime at Brighton. It was a surprise and delight to meet someone who knew the old haunts. He invited a whole crowd of Bluebell girls and my two skating friends Sylvaine and Claudette and myself to dinner. He had a lovely apartment not far from the Eiffel Tower. We were late back for the show and he drove us like a wild man through the crowded streets. Derek the manager was not pleased. 'Fifteen dollar fine for all of you!'

Harry was stunned, 'Look, I'll pay it. It's not fair to penalise them. It was my fault for keeping them.' Harry paid up like a man, kissed me on the cheek and said 'I'll see you after the show tonight. Come to the Lido again.'

We were there for nine weeks and towards the end, during the last two weeks, he invited me to save my money and move in to his spare bedroom. By then I felt quite close to him, felt I could trust him, and knew that he respected me. So I moved in to the lush apartment. There was one snag. I had decided to keep this to myself, but on the way out of the hotel at one o'clock – after everyone was safely in bed, so I thought, who should we meet at the front door, but the biggest gossip in the show. She looked at my suitcase, which Harry was carrying, and said pointedly, 'Oh, so you're leaving us?' The damage was done. It would be all over the cast within ten minutes of breakfast.

There came a moment in the next two weeks when, without much discussion we came to a mutual decision. On my part it was cold, calculated. I wanted the experience which others had flaunted before my eyes for so many years. Here, for the first time, I had met someone who could be trusted, who was experienced in the ways of the heart, and who cared for me genuinely, though I didn't fool myself that it was love.

This, of course, was 1963, when the permissive society was letting rip. Having nearly died in the accident just a few months before it had made me feel as if life was passing away and I knew nothing of it. Why shouldn't I have experiences like everyone else? So I felt no guilt.

My last memory of Harry is of our parting, at the Gare de Lyon. He grabbed a trolley from a stand. On it I went, with my three suitcases, for my trunk had been collected ahead of time, and he towed me to the train.

A quick kiss, a bouquet of fresh flowers were my parting gifts. We went out of each other's lives on a note of quiet understanding. There were no regrets, no remorseful feelings, and no pain.

12: Salute To Peace

Christmas was spent in Holland and was notable for the fact that my mother came out to visit me, and saw me perform on ice for the very first time. She was so proud.

Smoothing my black velvet leotard she said 'Ann, you're too skinny. I can see your rib cage.' And she bustled about with needle and thread, and had cups of tea ready at intervals, making sure that I and the other skaters were all right.

At the digs the stairs were very steep, typical of Dutch houses. Mum's car accident had affected her and I had to help her up with a hefty push from the rear. In our bedroom we shared some intimate conversations about things long gone – things which had hurt me at the time. It seemed as if this opportunity was being given to put it right. One night, sitting cross legged on my bed, in my nightie, watching her pour me a cup of tea I asked, 'Why did we have so many arguments when I was at home, Mum?' She came over to me with the tea. 'Arguments? I don't remember arguments. You are a funny girl.' And she pinched me on the cheek affectionately.

She said, 'I enjoyed the show tonight. Did you know that I was skating with you before you were born, and I was asked to go in an ice show at the height of my pregnancy. I still had a slim figure and it didn't show.' I stared at her, realising what I had never understood before . . . that grown-ups have reasons children know nothing of. I stored that thought for later exploration, and put my arms around her. 'Well, Mum, you have done very well with your dancing, haven't you?'

She brightened up a little, thinking of all her cups and medals and shields for ballroom dancing at home: 'Everybody has to have something, don't they?', she said, and I agreed, remembering the magic hours on the ice when my feet seemed to have wings as I glided, whirled and improvised to the music. That freedom was very different from the discipline of the chorus-line, when one had to submerge individuality.

She stayed two weeks, and we really enjoyed ourselves with concerts and sightseeing and nightclubs and shopping. She treated me to a pair of good Norwegian sealskin boots, so that my feet were no longer frozen by the Arctic blasts coming in from the sea, over the flatlands. When she left from Rotterdam airport, carrying the largest bunch of flowers I could purchase, she seemed to take away some of the light and joy and freedom of the past two weeks. I taxied back to my digs and got ready for the last show. Our next stop was to be Nuremberg, Germany and then it would be Eastern Europe.

On 16th January we found ourselves in the Sportovni Halle, in Prague, once the golden city of Europe. It was bitterly cold. Icicles dangled from the light standards in the street, and a grey mist, like fine snow in suspension, hung over the city. Derek Boyle, our manager, had given us words of advice before leaving the West, 'Expect your rooms to be bugged, and people to be watching you. Don't go out alone, and don't try to barter with the currencies because it's against the law and you will get yourself and the other person into trouble.' He added that we were not to sell or buy anything if people approached us in the streets. 'If you want to help them, give things away. . . .'

Half of our hotel bill was being paid (we cheered at this) and we were only getting one quarter of our salaries. The rest would be paid in dollars when we got out.

'Stock up on toilet things,' he told us. 'There's not a lot of that about there, and take some food in your trunk if you can. Oh – and watch what you say in the dressing room.'

'He's bringing me out in goose-bumps,' said Patsy, as we left the coffee bar. We remembered all this, however, when we found our hotel room in Prague. It was the last word in luxury – as its name, the Palace Hotel, implied. But I looked up at the crystal chandelier hanging in the centre of the ceiling and I wondered. Just then the phone rang. I picked it up, cautiously. 'Found any bugs, yet, Ann ?' asked Jack Graham.

'No, I've got my suspicions though. How do you find them?'

'I'll come up,' he said.

A minute or two later there was a knock on the door. Jack came in. 'Got a radio?' he mouthed. I handed him my clock radio. He turned it off station and held it up to the chandelier. We heard a humming noise. I fetched over a carved wood chair and he climbed up but could not reach. He dialled his room number and spoke briefly to Mike, his room-mate.

Soon I had the interesting experience of watching Mike balance on Jack's shoulders to reach the chandelier. Mike delicately picked out two bugs from the ceiling rose, and pulled down the main wire to which they were attached. After this, Jack went round the room and found two more behind the radiator.

'Is that it?' I asked. He nodded. 'I think you'll be all right now. This room's large enough for a party, Ann. How about it?' So later in the week, after the show we held a pancake party . . . the first of many.

Ted Shuffle, was nervily conscious of his responsibilities as choreographer to the very first American 'Holiday on Ice' show to visit Czechoslovakia. When we stepped out on the ice for our first rehearsal we gasped at the size of it . . . 15 headers long, no less.

Patsy muttered to me as we slid into our opening number, Black Velvet, 'I don't like this layout. The seats are too far back.' We felt that this would not create the warm, intimate atmosphere so necessary to a good performance. For the present we had other things to worry us . . . the attention of the photographers at rehearsals, for instance. There were about fifty of them, running around with lights, snapping us in our routines.

When we got to the Russian number Ted called for a departure from the order. 'Kim, Patsy, Ann and Jean stand by those curtains. Hold hands and look up.' We did and had a surprise. The curtains swished back. Herbert, an acrobatic star jumped from a balcony above us right over our heads in a split jump. It took all our training not to duck. 'Bravo!' shouted the photographers, after they had taken their pictures.

Our fears about the layout proved unfounded. There was a special atmosphere in that show . . . a tingle of expectancy in the air, and every seat taken. We offered them the best performance we could muster and the audience paid us back with their appreciation. At the finale, when we did the Queen Anne's Salute with the guns and flags of the world the audience stood and cheered to the echo, and stamped in time to the marching music. I had tears on my cheeks, because I felt that this was a cry for peace . . . a release of longing to express the things they could not say in any other way. I looked at Patsy and Maria, and they too had tears in their eyes. We stood there for a full 15 minutes, unable to get off the ice, waving at the crowds. It was quite cold to stand there but we stood, receiving that spontaneous warm tribute which thundered round the hall.

There were two interpreters with the show. We decided that one, Marisco by name, was trustworthy. He took us round Prague sightseeing, and we got to see King Charles Bridge and Castle Hadrian and the famous Gothic church, St Guy. The other man we suspected from the start. He kept looking through our mail. He approached Stephanie, our girl leader and asked 'Helen and Maria, where are they? Here are letters for them.' Stephanie looked startled. The girls named were Hungarian and Polish, and they had gained political asylum in Europe. They had stayed behind, for their own safety. Stephanie kept her presence of mind. 'They aren't in the show. They left long ago.' And she held out her hand for the letters. That seemed to shut him up and we heard no more about that. But it made us exceedingly wary of talking in his presence.

The dressers were all Czech and were supposed not to know English. We were warned, all the same, not to say too much about what we were going to do or where we had been in their presence. Carol forgot however, and showed us her new hairpiece. Barbara asked if she could get one as well. 'I got it from a hairdresser.' And she mentioned the name. Suddenly I saw this woman, who was supposed not to be able to speak English, listening. Sharply I said to her, 'Will you come and help me please.' She straightened up and came to me. A silence fell over the dressing room as the girls realised that she had understood my English request. Whether she was responsible or not, we didn't know, but the next time Carol went to the hairdresser he was not there.

But whatever the apparatus of the state, ordinary human kindness reached us. One morning I woke up with a swollen face – as big as a balloon. 'You must go to the clinic,' said the hotel doctor. But when we got there they would not touch it. 'You must go to the hospital,' they said, unwilling to take the responsibility. I wondered what I was in for. It couldn't have been worse.

The woman dentist at the hospital stood on an orange box to reach my mouth, and began to wave under my nose a pair of huge, steel Comic Cuts pliers, the kind my father used to take tacks out of boxes at home. I screamed and she said something very rude in Czech. Then she took a firm grip of the tooth with the pliers and yanked. I tried to get out of the chair but she had hemmed me in, well and truly. 'Anaesthetic!' I yelled.

Here my interpreter interposed. 'No anaesthetic!' he said abruptly, and left the room – to show sympathy, I presumed. Encouraged by the departure of this witness, the dentist took a fresh grip of the tooth, and went to work with all her might. The tooth came out in pieces, my lips were split. When she finally let me out of the chair I thought about punching her, but decided against it. I didn't fancy having to stay in jail over a dentist who would have made a better car mechanic. My one thought was to get out of this country as soon as possible. That night I couldn't skate in the show, and a piece appeared in the paper the next day: 'Smiler won't be in the show tonight.' People read about it and sent flowers, and messages of sympathy. I was quite touched, that these strangers would do this for me.

We were relieved to hear we were flying out, but the rumour went around that we were going on to Russia. Three of us did eventually, after a tour taking us to Copenhagen, Munster, Lille, Stockholm, Gothenburg, Oslo, and Reykjiavik. Finally I waved the rest of the cast goodbye and went on with Jean Sweetman and Monique to Leningrad, arriving on 5th May, 1964.

This new show was being assembled in exchange for the visit of the Russian circus to America. Therefore it had to have an all-American cast. I wasn't American but had skated in the USA and had clearance to work there. Besides I knew all the numbers.

Again there was the chance to make new friends. The first one was Darlene, my room mate. She was a terrific person, who spoke fluent Russian. This enabled us to escape from the Intourist guides and the dreary tours they organised, and get out among real Russian people.

Five days after arrival, and intensive rehearsals to polish up unfamiliar steps, we skated out on the ice to face our first Russian crowd. What an experience! To begin with we couldn't see them, because of the terrible glare from sixteen spotlights beaming down on the small square of ice, instead of the usual five or six. The audience were shielding their eyes with their programmes, poor things. The line of girls swung into the wheel and Dolly on the end of the line disappeared into the crowd of spectators, having lost her way in the dazzle. We were relieved to see her pick herself up and laugh with the audience.

Another hazard was that the orchestra had never seen such costumes before, and spent more time watching us than playing, that first night. They ignored Maurice, our French conductor, who travelled with us, and would fade in the most disconcerting way at the ends of bars, leaving us standing waiting for the next musical cue. It was downright embarrassing, especially as we had a five-star audience, which included diplomats, ambassadors, Soviet government officials – and the Kirov ballet company. Afterwards the girls from the Kirov came backstage to greet us and they apologised for the orchestra. 'We were so sad for you. How could they spoil your show like that?' They were almost crying. Ted Shuffle snapped, 'We've got to have rehearsals tomorrow for those musicians or I'll wring their necks. Imagine, with all those important people in the audience, and we were made to look like idiots. . . .'

Off-stage we were subjected to the constant and subtle pressure of ordinary Russians who wanted to get hold of American records or clothes. We met it everywhere . . . amongst the crowds of youngsters besieging the stage doors, in the lifts going up to our rooms. Even the cleaners in the hotel would ask if we had any clothes they could buy. I gave a blue wool suit to one of these. Next day she brought a fistful of roubles to my room, which I refused to take. She cried and told me, through Darlene, that her husband was in prison. 'She says she has never met such generosity,' said Darlene.

We ate mainly in the hotel dining room and the food was terrible. No oranges, no milk in our coffee, very few vegetables, beetroot for breakfast, mashed potato with every meal, and the meat tasted foul. 'What animal is this?' I asked the waiter, through Darlene. He shrugged expressively. 'Rats,' Bob said with an evil grin and we all pushed our plates away.

We tried other hotels but the diet was just as boring. In the end I incurred gingivitus of the gums and Derek Boyle asked the interpreter to obtain lots of oranges. I had to sit and eat these luscious golden treats while the rest of the cast struggled with their yoghurt.

I couldn't shake off a sense of being watched. One day I was talking to a lady lift operator in the hotel, and she was asking me for clothing when a voice intruded into our conversation, speaking in Russian. Whatever the message through the hidden microphone she understood it too well, for she stopped the lift sixteen floors below mine and bundled me out, looking terribly frightened, and I had to walk the rest of the way up.

13: Danger Ride

We skated three shows a day nearly every day for three months, on a minimal diet. Five people were hospitalised and the rest of us worn to a frazzle.

The weather undoubtedly had unsettled us with its rapid changes. In April we encountered the icy grip of winter in Leningrad. In Moscow, a month later, summer bloomed along the banks of the river Volga, and Russian families were enjoying the White Night, when midnight was like day. Kiev in June and July was ripe with luscious fruit, which helped us, though we still couldn't get decent meat, or the protein we needed, in view of the energy we expended. Still, the people seemed sunnier and more open towards us. One day we woke up to beautiful music, and looking out of our windows saw children in national costume performing Ukrainian folk dancing in the town square. They were practising for a competition to be held in the local theatre that afternoon. Hundreds of boys and girls had come from all over the Ukraine to compete. I grabbed my movie camera and recorded it. Darlene spoke to the right person and she, Dolores and I were given an invitation to the performance. We were sitting enjoying the spectacle when a voice spoke in our ears, in quite good English. 'Do not look around. We noticed you yesterday watching the ballet, and we would like to meet you in person. Could you meet us at three o'clock at the main post office?'

We did glance round quickly and it was two good-looking chaps we had seen the day before at the ballet. Naturally, therefore, we hurried to keep the appointment.

At the post office they had a car ready and we jumped in. So began a friendship which enlivened our month's stay in Kiev. Through our two Ukrainian friends, who were scientists, we were able to move about among ordinary families, and see how they really lived.

The impression left on us was of a country twenty years behind the times. In the homes we saw, there was little privacy and no luxuries, no baths, no carpets. People were afraid to be overheard grumbling, and would go out in the streets and walk up and down, talking. 'It is the only safe way,' explained Ivan, one of our scientists. 'There is a lack of trust. People report on each other to the police.'

In Moscow we had visited Lenin's tomb, and seen his waxy face under a glass cover. Ordinary people queued for an eternity, inching forward to kiss the glass. Tourists jumped the queue. 'Why do they worship him like that,' I asked. 'He's dead, isn't he?' Oleg said seriously, 'Lenin lives on in his teaching.' But he gave me the impression he didn't believe it.

They wanted to know about Europe, and told us that the papers gave little news. What there was they tended not to believe unless confirmed by Western radio stations. Oleg took us to a shop where books of disinformation about the West were being sold, and we took some away with us.

That friendship was a highlight of our stay in the Soviet Union. Darlene was crying as our plane took off. We had glimpsed them in the crowd at the airport, then they had melted out of sight. 'I wonder if we'll ever see them again?' I mused aloud. 'I'm going to keep in touch,' Darlene exclaimed still moist-eyed.

Most of the Americans were going home, but I was down for another European tour. Already in Paris, learning the numbers, were girls from other Europe and Far East tours.

Because I was tired I was given two weeks off and could go home for a break. Portslade looked just the same, and Mum and Dad were so happy to see me. It was lovely meeting old friends, but I was amazed at how many of them were married. There were only two of us from our old class still single. Still, I went dancing, and met a detective, and played tennis with Dad, and went for car drives and generally got back to normal.

I was glad that Dad's position was improving. He was now a director of Greenfields, the furniture removal company, and we also had our own personal furniture shop, which Mum managed. She had taken on a new lease of life, though it was hard work.

So I went to join the company in Paris feeling refreshed – with lots of ideas as to how to make life interesting. In Holland I hired a coach and arranged a tulip tour for the cast. I met a dishy German architect called Erkhardt, who thereafter kept popping up in every city we visited. He eventually proposed marriage to me in Barcelona, but by then I had gone off men rather badly. All because of an incident that took place in Zaratoga, Spain.

Sandy and I were invited to dinner with a Moroccan diplomat whom we met at the hotel where most of the cast were staying. I went to change, and when I came back Sandy, looking rather odd, brushed past me, murmuring, 'I have another date, Ann. See you later.' I stood looking after her, wondering where she had acquired a date so quickly. Then Juan took my arm and said smoothly, in French, 'You look charming.'

As an escort he was passable, being tall and well-built, well-dressed and comfortably middle-aged, with a politely pleasant manner. We had a drink at the bar and he went to make a phone call. He was away rather a long time and I was beginning to feel a sense of disquiet. When he returned, his manner had changed. He seemed put out about something. He grabbed my arm and said 'Let's go,' almost hustling me out of the bar.

Once in the car, a Volkswagen, he began to drive out of

the city, very fast. This went on for some time, and what with that and the silence of my host my sense of unease was growing more insistent. At last I said, 'Will we be getting to the restaurant soon?'

His answer came as a shock: 'No, I am going to rape you.' It was so absurd, I laughed. But his next words wiped the smile from my face: 'I mean it.' Gone was the polite smoothness. He was tense, brusque and sweating profusely. I wondered if he was under the influence of drugs.

'Over my dead body.' I said it without thinking, and it was not a very sensible reply, given the circumstances, but my mind was busy with plans of escape from this dilemma. Should I humour him?

'Now come on,' I said. 'You're upset about something, but don't take it out on me. Let's stop somewhere to eat.'

At that he got into a frenzy. 'I am going to do it. As soon as I find a place I will do it.'

I decided to use my parachute training (acquired on a half day in Skegness) and fall out. I opened the door and prepared to go, but the next minute I was grabbed in a powerful grip, and the door was slammed in my face. The car meanwhile was continuing on a straight course. The next thing I knew was that I was looking down the barrel of a handgun.

I sat frozen with fear, my mind working overtime. He would have to stop soon, and that might give me an opportunity.

I could just see my watch by the headlights. It was after eleven o'clock. The car was slowing down. We seemed to be in an open space, with no recognisable features, nor lights. He switched off the engine and the lights and, getting out of the car, walked away a little distance, I presumed to relieve himself. But he had left the keys in the ignition.

Here was my chance. I switched over to the driving seat and tried to start the car. There was a terrific grinding of gears, and to my horror, when I pressed the accelerator to go forwards the car jerked backwards, hitting my assailant, and knocking him over.

I switched into another gear and drove forward, but as I gathered speed Juan wrenched open the door on the driver's side, and jumped in, throwing me into the back seat of the car in one movement. Somehow, I arrived sitting upright. How I didn't break my neck I shall never know. The man was so powerful, and under the influence of drugs.

Juan brought the car to a halt, got out once more and came in beside me, I was petrified with fear, but my resistance was not over. I argued with him, in my best English school-marm manner.

'You are on drugs, aren't you? You need help. You won't get it this way.'

Then an inspiration came to me. He had been a long time on the phone – perhaps he had borrowed the car. 'This isn't your car, is it?' I asked. 'No, it is not my car. It belongs to a friend. What of it?' he rapped out.

I made up a story about having had an abortion and that it would cause a lot of bleeding if he should assault me. I hoped his medical knowledge didn't extend to knowing about such things.

He paused, and thought. It was obvious he didn't fancy it. We sat there in silence for a while. Then, quite suddenly, as if a switch had been thrown, he returned to his normal self. The man I had met in the hotel was there again. He got out of the back seat with a muttered apology and we drove back to town in silence. It was two o'clock in the morning when we arrived at the apartment where I was staying.

When I got out of the car I couldn't walk; I tottered like a drunkard, with no strength to even stand up. He escorted me up in the lift – holding me upright, since my knees had turned to jelly. Then he left me at the door of the apartment, with a whispered warning: 'Don't tell the police!'

I fell against the door and the family with whom I was

staying came out to find me in a heap on the floor. In hysterical bursts I told them what had happened. They tried to soothe me and calm my distress. 'In the morning we must go to the police,' they said, and put me to bed.

But in the morning another ordeal awaited me – being examined. The police were very kind and very concerned, because I was a guest in their country. To think this had happened to one of the 'Holiday on Ice' cast – it was unthinkable! The police doctor found me badly bruised from having been thrown into the back seat, but with no worse physical injury.

Acting on the information I gave them the police took me to the hotel, to interview the manager, since Juan had been staying there when I met him. The manager was all concern. 'I told him to go yesterday morning. Then in the evening I find that he is still here, and that you have been seen going out of the door with him. It is very bad.' I learned that Juan was a chauffeur, not a diplomat, and that he was wanted for possessing narcotics, which he had tried to post through a hotel porter. The police had intercepted the package, since they had had this man under surveillance for some time.

Then the manager said something even more startling. 'Didn't your friend warn you about him?'

'What friend?' I couldn't think what he meant.

'The friend who was with you. My head waiter warned her not to go out with this dangerous man.'

My anger rose. So Sandy had known of his character. She had made a lame excuse and rushed off, without warning me. If she had walked in at that moment there might have been a nasty scene. I wanted to beat her up. I had always looked after her interests.

The upshot of it was that the manager offered me the best room in the hotel for as long as the ice show was there. It was a beautiful suite, with my own bathroom. But I was not destined to stay there alone. Monica came bursting in and refused to leave me. I protested that I was all right, but when I tried to get out of bed I just fell over. My legs would

99

not work. There was no skating for the next four days.

Sandy came to see me and began to cry all over me.

'Stop it. Get her out of here,' I yelled. The thought of forgiveness was very far away from me. If only she had warned me.

This incident left its mark. For a long time I didn't go anywhere alone. And it affected my attitude to men. When Erkhardt asked me to marry him in Barcelona I refused. I was still shocked and felt I could not trust a man now.

The episode was not completely finished. Three months later I was sitting in a restaurant in Madrid, with Monica. It was packed, and I had a clear view of the door. We were talking and laughing over the menu when I found my attention drawn to a couple who had just walked in. It was Juan, with a good-looking woman.

Monica noticed that I had gone white. 'What's the matter?' she asked. I said faintly, 'It's that man . . . here.' She looked round and saw Juan. At the same instant he recognised me, and a look of fright crossed his face. As I went one way to the telephone, Juan and the woman went the other way, out of the back door. By the time the police arrived there was no sign of them, though the police spent a long time scouring the city. As for me I was badly shaken up and made to feel that he would always be doing this – breaking into my life.

When I could think clearly about the experience I was glad that I had been able to keep my cool and act with decision. Above all it convinced me that Someone Up There was watching over me, real good.

In the early part of '67, after five long years on tour in Europe, the show visited England. We did two weeks each in Leicester and Cardiff and my mother came to Leicester with a cake for a party on 23rd February, my twenty-eighth birthday. We would not be seeing each other for a long time. The show was off to Japan and the Far East for a year.

Before that, however, we fitted in a tour round

Scandinavia. It reminded me of Canada, with its brilliant blue lakes contrasting with deep white snow, and red reeds growing beside rivers, and abundant wild life.

As the cast were piling into a coach in Vasteras, Sweden, Chris, one of the boys, suddenly called out, 'Hey, look. There's Marcele Marceau.'

'Oh, where?' I was instantly alert. I had seen this famous mime artist on television and admired his art tremendously. Besides, a friend of mine, Richard Knight had been a student of his for a short time.

'Oh dear,' said David, 'She's off again. . . . She never misses a trick.'

I pushed past the people getting on and landed beside the great Marceau. Without make-up I wouldn't have recognised him.

'I'm Ann Terry from 'Holiday on Ice', and this is our coach. I really admire your gifts of mime, from one artist to another. Will you ever be coming to England again?'

He looked at me with those marvellous mobile features and said, 'One of my favourite places is Brighton.'

'That's where my home is!' I cried, in delight.

'If I am ever there, you come and look me up.' He spoke beautiful, mellifluous English.

Twelve years later I rang him up at the Metropole Hotel. Somehow he remembered my voice and my name and asked me to meet him at the stage door of the Theatre Royal. There he handed me two tickets for the front row of the stalls. That, I thought, was real class.

14: East Is East

We opened in Korakeun Ice Palace, Tokyo, on 9th June, 1967, after four days' rehearsal. The bustling streets were hot, sticky and smelly from the open drains, but were frequently sprayed by masked sanitary workers. Inside the Ice Palace, however, the ice engineers had worked their miracle, laying down an Olympic-sized sheet of ice.

The star of the show, Miwa, a Japanese amateur champion, in her first professional ice show, was dainty and precise in her movements, dancing across the ice like a butterfly in her yellow, sequinned dress which gathered up the radiance of the spotlights. Because of Miwa, the press took a special interest in all of us.

She came from a wealthy family, and her parents invited us to a big party at their home. They bowed politely to us, and we bowed back, awkwardly. There was an etiquette to follow in the precise degree of the bow. It was difficult to tell what the Japanese were thinking. Their mask-like inscrutability really unnerved me.

I thought I was a very patient person until I got to Japan, but the way they did things really amazed me. I went to a small store to buy some Kleenex on my way to rehearsals. The woman behind the counter insisted on wrapping the small box as if it were a precious gift. I explained I was in a hurry but she wouldn't listen, so I tried to take it away from her and we had an undignified tug of war which I lost. Without the least change of expression, or word of reproach the woman finished tying the package and handed it over with the correct shop assistant's bow . . . very low.

I felt exasperated, as I hurried away. 'You just can't win here,' I told the girls at the show, explaining my lateness. Another annoying Japanese trait was their habit of laughing behind their hands so as not to show their teeth – that was considered bad form.

You couldn't get very far in Japan without shedding your shoes. When you entered a hotel, you had to leave them at the door, and put on a pair of slippers that the mama-san would give you. Then, at the door of your room you shed those slippers and went in barefoot.

Many were the hassles when we wanted to go to the bathroom. It was slippers off again and you stepped down into the bathroom, in wooden clogs.

There were other funny customs, like the wearing of kimonos, and communal bathing. I was not in favour of that, and used to put the latch down, so I could have the big pool to myself. It was usually piping hot, and I would gently lower myself, turning beetroot red an inch at a time, while angry crowds gathered at the door, demanding entrance.

Our clothes were not put in the cupboards in our rooms, but over wooden clothes horses. The cupboards were used for the bedding rolls, produced at night. These rooms were sitting-rooms during the day, and at night you could find yourself sharing with anyone, of either sex. I didn't like this idea very much so I paid more to have a room on my own.

About four days into the show we received a surprise visit from Emperor Hirohito and the Empress Nagko, the representatives of a dynasty stretching back unbroken for more than 2,400 years. When he came to the throne, in 1926, the Emperor was hailed as divine, the 24th Imperial Son of Heaven. Here he was, now 66, and definitely human, enjoying our show, as far as one could tell. We lined up back stage, after the finale, to be presented.

The royal couple were escorted around the edge of the ice to meet the stars first and be given flowers. Suddenly, right in front of me, the Emperor slipped. Before anyone else could lift a finger I moved like lightning, stepped forward and grabbing him by the arm, steadied him so that he did not fall. The inscrutable Japanese face turned to me, and broke into a smile. He acknowledged me with a slight bow and an English 'Thank-you'. The party moved on. 'Quick work,' said Betsy with a sideways smile, but I was in a fine sweat. One just didn't lay ordinary, peasant hands on an emperor. In the dressing room afterwards the other girls assured me that it would have caused terrible loss of face all round if he had fallen.

About a week into the show, during the hill-billy number I had an accident. Jackie Graham, dressed up as a man, pulled the trigger of a rifle, and with the bang we all went flat on our backs on the ice, as if dead. When the cast arose, I couldn't, but lay spread-eagled on the ice with a pulled ligament in my knee.

That put me out of the show for seven weeks. I couldn't afford my apartment since I was on half-pay. Friends came to my aid and so while the show went on to the next town, I remained in Tokyo with them. The husband was the editor of a Tokyo newspaper.

Through this couple I obtained an interview with a Buddhist priest. It came about through a discussion as we sat round the dining table. (Their home was half Japanese style and half Western. My bed was a proper one, and I was grateful).

That day I had seen some processions in the streets which were gaudy, noisy and strange, with hundreds of women running to kiss a huge phallic symbol as it was carried along by priests. A little embarrassed I asked why the women did that.

'That's because they want a healthy boy child,' said Amano with a grin that split his impassive mask for a moment.

'And does it work?' I asked cheekily, and the little Japanese ladies round the table put their hands over their mouths and tee-heed in that silly Mikado style.

I mentioned the festival I had seen at Nagasaki, where

men and women took lights and floated them away on the water, till they passed from sight.

'That is for the spirits of dead. We believe that they come back at this festival and we send out a light to welcome them.'

I listened solemnly to this. Nagasaki stood out in my mind, since it was a place of death. Strange as it may seem, I did not know about the atomic bombs which had wiped out that city and Hiroshima, ending Japan's involvement in the Second World War. I was five then – and had somehow escaped learning the details since. So I endured sullen sideways looks from the Japanese in a puzzled silence, as I went round the museum, until a friend with me interpreted what the notices said, and I felt sick.

A few days later, as a result of this conversation, Conn, Amano's wife and her tiny friend Michiko-san took me in a taxi to the biggest temple in Tokyo, where I met a Buddhist priest.

He led us to a room, and we sat on tatami matting. We were supposed to kneel, but because I couldn't kneel they gave me a chair without legs, and bolstered me with cushions. In came a graceful Japanese girl in a kimono, and a big black obi who with great delicacy performed the tea ceremony. Every move was pregnant with meaning, and in the end she handed us thin cups into which she had poured and whisked the green tea.

That over with, the Buddhist priest turned to me: 'I understand you have many questions about our way of life in Japan?' he said pleasantly. He was a young man, and he was out to enjoy this encounter with a foreign lady who would ask blunt foreigner's questions.

'What does the tea ceremony mean?' I started with a quickie, as I thought. But it turned out to take half an hour to answer. We progressed to women's place in society. 'They don't seem to have much freedom,' I said tentatively. 'The woman's place is in the home,' he said with a certainty that annoyed me.

Inevitably we arrived at God. Somehow, he was never

far from my conversations round the world. Tentatively I drew on my memories of the creed, learned at my church school: 'The God in England, he is three in one. We have God the Father, his Son Jesus and the Holy Spirit. What does this Buddha represent?'

The priest sketched for me an outline of the philosophy of his religion. I found it very complicated and rather unintelligible. I said, 'The God that I want to believe in is not like that. He is not a statue. He is a supernatural being, and I believe that he is alive. He created the universe, and is not limited, in any way.'

We left on friendly terms and I found to my surprise that four hours had passed. Going out, my friends Conn and Michiko-san said, 'We are glad you asked all those questions. We would never have dared to, and now we understand our religion. We never did before . . . and do you know, we no longer believe it. It does not make sense.' I looked at my tiny Japanese companions and felt as if God had moved nearer. Was I looking for him – or was he looking for me?

When the tour moved on to Koshi in the northern island, I stayed in a hotel that had originally been a palace. It was very old, and my room was huge, like a banqueting hall, with silk wallpaper and oriental decoration. Mercifully it had its own bathroom – with a shower but no bath. For that I had to troop down two flights of stairs to the communal bath – and I barred myself in, while people outside tried to break down the door.

Coming back to the room that first day I went to get my skates – and saw a strange ornament fixed to the wall, by my bag. I didn't think it unusual, as in Japan pictures were often at low level. This was clay-coloured, and had spokes which spread out all around it, and it was the size of a dinner plate. 'My,' I thought to myself, as I went towards my bag, 'I wouldn't have anything like that on my wall. I must have it taken out.'

Suddenly the thing on the wall blinked at me. I jumped back. It was a tarantula spider . . . now I recognised it from a book I had read in Portslade Library. I just hadn't been prepared to find one in my bedroom. I grabbed the telephone and shouted for help. The maid came. She was wizened and lined but obviously quite agile and ready to cope with such emergencies. Taking off her shoe she advanced on the thing. The spider knew what she was going to do. It leaped over my bag and scuttled out of the door and down the corridor. She followed, throwing her slipper at it, until eventually she clouted it. Then she scooped up the carcase with a pair of tongs and scuttled away, a little like the spider herself.

In Fukuoko I had a nasty encounter with a Japanese gang-leader. I didn't know who he was at the time or I would have handled the situation with more tact. 'Will you please leave my table!' I commanded the oily-looking Japanese with the scarred face who boldly came and sat down beside me when my escort went to make a call. Scarface looked daggers, but left. Then Tami, my Indonesian escort returned and said in a stage whisper, 'Let's get out of here. There are some dangerous men here. I've seen knives on them.'

We hurried to the door, only to come face to face with Scarface and his gang. They shouted threateningly and the leader went for me. Suddenly, viciously, he lashed out, karate-style, kicking me in the stomach. I doubled up in agony. The next few minutes were rather confused. A taxi pulled up. I got in. The gang-leader got in after me. I managed to kick him out. Then I called Tami to get in the cab. He was trying to placate the gang, telling them, 'Look she is English. She is a guest in your country. What do you think you are doing? She is with the ice show.' The next minute I heard apologies from the gang. It appeared that their leader was drunk; that he had lost face when I turned him down. I was in too much pain to care. 'Get me to the hospital,' I told the taxi driver. Tami at last got in and we drove off.

At the hospital they found no broken bones, only bad bruising, and gave me pain killers, warning me that my metabolism might be upset for a while. It was. I missed a performance, and was far from comfortable for months after.

I kept bumping into missionaries. In Tokoshima I went to buy a dress in a clothes store and found myself tugging it from the grasp of an American woman, who recognised I was English. She turned out to be a pastor's wife.

Mrs Carpenter invited me home to lunch and to her church. There was a small congregation, and her husband explained to me that it was very hard to work in Japan, where Buddhism and Shintoism had firm hold. I was grateful for the chance to eat Western style, being very tired of eating raw or half-cooked carrots, cabbages and potatoes. And I had rice coming out of my ears. Even the cakes were made of rice flour. They were a pleasant couple and I was grateful that they did not push their religious beliefs at me. I admired them for putting up with all the inconveniences of living in Japan, so far from home.

'Why do you do it?' I asked.

'We have a calling,' they said. It sounded mysterious, but important. I let the matter drop.

Through Mrs Carpenter I met a lot of people who invited me home. I was a novelty . . . someone fresh to talk to. Besides, I could get them complimentary tickets to see the show.

One day I went to tea with Elizabeth, an English lady married to a Japanese doctor, Dr Itchihara. I was intrigued by their marriage as I had gathered that women were third-class in this part of the world. But she seemed more than well treated, even treasured, and proclaimed herself happy – except for the fact that she saw very little of her husband, because he worked hard day and night.

'We fell in love at university in England,' she explained. 'He invited me out to Japan for a holiday, and I decided to stay.' She also told me that she had given up her medical studies to marry Itchihara, and that it had taken her seven years to learn Japanese properly. She seemed happy enough, with her three children, and her nice home. She

108

also taught English and had learned ikebana flower arranging. I could see that she had married not just a man but a whole culture. I wouldn't have liked to live where she did, right out in the country. There was a touch of wistfulness about her expression as she told me that she had not been back to England since her marriage. 'I sometimes think that if I went back I would not return,' she said gently, 'I have had to make so many adjustments to live here.'

One of my happiest memories is of what happened when we arrived on an island late at night, with a show next day and nowhere to sleep. Erica, Mariana, Patsy and I all piled into a taxi and asked the driver to take us to a hotel. But they were all full.

'I know what we'll do. I will take you to my pastor,' said the Japanese driver, smiling. To my surprise he introduced us to a charming American couple, the Hoaglunds. They persuaded a member of their church who owned a hotel to find a room for us. The whole episode stuck in my memory, not only for the trouble everyone went to, but for the love that streamed out to us from them. I kept in touch afterwards. Friends like that are more precious than rubies.

15: Down Under

From Japan we went to Hong Kong, where we stayed for a month. I bought a carved rosewood chest, lined with camphorwood, and piled it high with presents for the family . . . cashmere sweaters, beaded purses, and a chess set made of ivory. Then a shipping company packed it off to Portslade to arrive in time for Christmas.

Hong Kong was in a state of civil unrest over the raising of the bus fares, as I remember, and we heard bomb explosions. We ice-skated in a football stadium under the stars, and our changing rooms were made of canvas, which didn't protect us from the weather. The November climate was unpredictable. Sometimes it would be sunny and then the ice melted, or it would rain, and the ice melted. Either way we got a lot of time off. If we managed to get through the first half we got paid. If we had to stop during the first half the audience got its money back, and we didn't get paid. Well, we tried, but sometimes, after an hour our skates would be cutting through sludge, or we would be down to the pipes, which was dangerous. Imagine doing an adagio, being lifted by your partner above his head, or doing the death spin, held by one hand only and with your head touching the ice – then running out of of ice. . . .

We arrived in Manila in mid-December. At Areneta's Coliseum, Quezon City, a new suburb of Manila where our show was situated, the first sign that greeted us was 'Please Leave Your Guns Here', instead of the more usual 'Please Leave Your Coats'. It was indeed a dangerous place. When you hailed a cab, the commissionaire of the hotel noted your name, the number of the cab, and your destination, for security reasons. So many Americans had been robbed, and dumped out of town, miles from anywhere, that the tourist department was taking no chances, for fear of an exodus of foreigners and their currency.

A company bus was laid on to take the skaters in and out of town to their hotels, but I chose to stay near the Areneta, in a first-class hotel. It was surrounded by trees, and immaculate waiters serving drinks round the pool. Through staying there I met influential men, who used it for prestige lunches and dinners. We had our press party there as well, and the upshot of all this was that I had the use of several chauffeur-driven limousines to take me shopping.

In the market I met Connie, the owner of a gift shop, where I bought craft items in shell and hand-carved wood. Connie turned out to be a gem; she took a real liking to me and invited me to her home for Christmas, to meet her husband and family. 'Have you seen very much of the Philippines yet?' she asked. I admitted I hadn't. 'Well, get your friends together and we'll do a day tour,' she announced. That tour ended with a barbecue, out on a beach, where we ate fish cooked over a driftwood fire, and swallowed oysters.

On another day Connie asked me if I had ever shot the rapids on a world-famous river, whose name I forget. She said, 'Well, we'll do it. I've always wanted to.' It turned out to be quite a ride. The river was fast-flowing and very rocky. The canoes could have easily turned over but for the consummate skill of the canoeists, who, in places, jumped out and steered the boats over the rocks.

Before I spent Christmas with Connie, I went to church, with Corsino, a young Filipino airline steward, whom I had met at the hotel. This church held services in three languages – Spanish, Chinese and English. Unfortunately

I picked the wrong time and found myself in the Chinese service. I couldn't understand a word, but I did notice that the bamboo organ made beautiful music. Corsino told me that to keep the bamboo from being eaten by termites, they buried it in the sand for a couple of years until it was thoroughly impregnated with salt.

I had a surprise visitor one night at the show. Betty, from the Wizard of Oz days in London, came backstage after the performance, with her mother and a babe in arms. 'When did you get married?' I asked, surprised. She was the last person I expected to see there. Her beautiful face, which reminded me of Elizabeth Taylor, looked sad, and out came a story of misguided love and betrayal. She wanted to get back to England and hoped to get into the show.

I spoke to Derek, the manager, but he felt that as she hadn't skated for a while she'd be out of practice. 'As you know, Ann, being one of the oldest skaters in the show, most of the cast are youngsters and you have to be physically fit to keep up with them.' I nodded. I was fit, but I knew what he meant. Betty was an excellent skater in the Wizard of Oz, but her situation would be too complicated for a travelling show. So when I met her a couple of days later I told her, tactfully, what Derek had said. 'I half expected it.' She gave a thin smile.

At a New Year party given for the cast by Areneta, the governor of that area, I looked round the very merry crowd assembled at the poolside and a feeling of misgiving hit me hard. Perhaps the conversation with Betty was still having an effect, but I realised that my days in this job were numbered. The world's most glamorous job? Certainly it was. A lot of fun? Yessir. But I was twenty-nine – and there were no more goals I could achieve in skating. Round the pool the glittering new generation of skaters laughed and joked. The world was theirs. But there were also the oldsters, some of whom hit the bottle to give themselves confidence to get on the ice. I didn't want to end like that. 'What am I doing here?' I thought.

Looking for congenial company I spied Jackie, the star of the show, sitting at a table with her parents who had just arrived from England. The lights round the swimming pool made reflections on the water as I walked over to them. Jackie smiled at me. 'Ann, what's the matter? You look really down in the dumps.'

'It's New Year's Eve, and I wish I were at home. I want to give up travelling.' Yet even as I said it I knew I didn't want a boring life, only one more stable – and with a future.

Jackie's parents were very warm folk. 'We thought you lapped it up, and were enjoying everything. What's this about you shooting the rapids?', they asked.

Just then the clowns dived spectacularly into the water. Everyone laughed and the mood changed. Herman came up to me. 'Ann, are you hot?'

'I sure am,' I replied.

'Right!' And he swept me up in his arms and dumped me in the pool. My hair piece came off and with my white evening dress clinging to me, I made a quick exit, to applause.

'Ann, the good sort, who could take it.' That was my reputation.

From Manila we flew to Sydney, Australia, into the sun all the way. We were given special eye-shades so that we could sleep. I didn't waste time sleeping . . . I went into the cockpit to meet the captain.

We toured for six months in Australia playing in Sydney, Melbourne, Adelaide, Brisbane and Perth. I felt safe and able to relax. Australians were terribly casual about everything, particularly dress, wearing shorts for work, even in the banks, because it was so hot. It was disconcerting to dress up for a date and find that he had dressed down, in shorts and sneakers.

The country gave the impression of being in the

making. Sydney was like a beach town and there was the great Opera House, under construction, dominating the skyline.

Australian men were real men – they ate steak for breakfast! It was a world where sport was king – you name it, they played it . . . cricket, tennis, wrestling, surfing. One day, basking on a rock after swimming on Bondi beach we heard a terrible scream, and turned to see a white turmoil in the water below, where a shark had taken a bather. I had to turn away, wanting to vomit.

Wherever we went we skated on frozen tennis courts which could be relied on to be flat, with the necessary seating capacity. We left our trademark at the Melbourne courts where Davis Cup matches were played, when the brine leaked through and burnt the grass.

At a sports party I met the Fraser brothers, tennis stars of my youth, also Bobby Cowper and Jackie Gleason, spin bowlers who played at Lords that year. It was a nice change to meet clean-cut sportsmen. They were a lot of fun and we went out together in a group with their wives, after shows.

I had a pen-pal of some sixteen years' standing, and his parents paid my plane fare to their farm in Blue Mountains. My five-day stay was full of interest. Emus snatched my bag of crisps, bush babies gave me their fleas. Touring the ranch by jeep we drove at a snail's pace to avoid the kangaroos, which suddenly leaped out from behind hedges. A seven-feet long iguana lizard climbed a tree and changed colour before my eyes.

The next step was Singapore. At the airport a nasty shock awaited us. Derek Boyle got on an orange box and called us together. 'I'm sorry, I haven't got the money to pay your salaries, not even a sub,' he announced. We looked at each other, aghast. We had all without exception, taken the opportunity, during six months in Australia, to put our salaries in the bank, transferring them home. We had expected a sub at the airport to help us through till payday, a few days later. Derek went on, 'We've had to send Heinz back to Australia for a part that's broken down on the ice machine. You'll have to make your own way to town, and find your own accommodation.'

How could a cast of seventy-five live for the week it would take to repair the machine, without any money? It occurred to me that we should pool our cash, and I was talking this over with one or two of the men when a passenger, to whom I had been chatting on the plane appeared.

'I heard that announcement. That's really terrible. What can I do to help?' he enquired solicitously.

'I need to get to town, somehow, and find somewhere to stay, and I haven't enough to last me till the end of the week.'

'You must come with me. Bring a few of your friends. My limousine will be waiting outside.'

It certainly was waiting outside – and halfway down the street, being enormously long and sleek. He had to be someone important. Half a dozen of us piled in. 'Good old Ann. She's done it again,' whispered the girls as we set off.

We asked our friend if he could recommend a hotel that was reasonable and not too far from the ice rink. Over the telephone in his car he phoned around for us and located a reasonable, clean, apartment hotel. (I found out its drawback later: opera at 6.30am.) Rooms were sixteen dollars, but I managed to get a single room for twelve.

Meanwhile some of the others had not fared so well. Two days later I learned from a friendly lady at the hotel that a few of the girls were staying in a brothel on the other side of town. She had more to say. 'Are you aware that the owner of this hotel is charging his business friends fifty dollars for an introduction to you? You are going out to dinner rather a lot aren't you?'

I nodded. I had been glad of these invitations as I didn't have the money to buy my meals.

'Well,' my friend went on, 'They're paying him for the prestige of your company. It clinches their deals.'

Was I furious! But I thought of a way of teaching him a lesson. At the end of the week, when I got my bill, I deducted half of the owner's takings for each evening's date from my own bill. This left me with nothing to pay him. He was really annoyed. I had made him look a fool. I stayed on though, since it was a way of getting in touch with influential people. And a few friends were always useful to a single, unprotected young lady.

The tour finished in Kuala Lumpur, Malaya. On the plane the nice man sitting next to me turned out to be a government minister.

'I'm fed up with travelling,' I told him. 'I'm longing to get home, and give up show business.'

He picked up my hand and turned it palm up. 'From what I see young lady you've got a few more years to go before you hang up your skates.'

'Oh no. I'll be in my thirties,' I thought. 'If this goes on, I'll be the first old-age pensioner on ice.'

I enjoyed staying, not in a hotel, but with Malayan friends of Pat Pritchard from Nottingham. She had said goodbye to the show in Leicester, to marry a Dutch engineer, passing on all her hotel addresses, and the address of these friends, to me.

The Malayan families I met were really generous, giving me beautiful presents such as a crocodile handbag. I swam, played golf, and sun-bathed in the garden, keeping a weather eye open for the naughty chimpanzees, playing in the trees. The leader would become very spiteful at intruders in what he regarded as his private world. So there was little chance of relaxing with a good book.

We flew back to England on a troop carrier, via New Delhi, Frankfurt, and Paris. It took twenty-eight agonising hours, jammed like sardines in a real bone-shaker of a plane.

Some people we would never see again in 'Holiday on

Ice'. Others were joining new shows. In my hand was a contract for Israel and Europe, and for all my dislike of travelling around, I was glad of it. At least I would be going somewhere different, and perhaps Israel, centre of the world's greatest drama, would have a few answers for me.

16: Humble Pie

After one month's holiday it was time to be off again to Israel. Dad drove me out to Heathrow, and on the way we talked about some of my adventures in the Far East.

'It was a wise thing to make your will,' Dad said. 'Mum's renewed the insurance on your legs.' He spoke as if my fate were sealed. My disposable estate consisted of one movie camera, one piece of real estate in Deltona, Florida, all the beautiful gold jewellery I bought in Portugal and Germany, and my stamp collection. They would go to the family if anything happened to me. It gave me a peculiar peace of mind, seeing to my wordly affairs like this.

Approaching the airport I said to Dad, 'I wonder if I'll know anyone in the cast. I'll need a room mate. Israel is expensive.'

He laughed. 'You'll know someone. You've never been short of friends yet.'

We were meeting by the Air Israel desk and immediately I spotted Kimber, a tall elegant ex-Bluebell girl from the Lido in Paris, now a skater. She smiled at Dad. 'So you're leaving Ann with us again, are you?'

'I think we can spare her for another year,' Dad laughed.

Another voice said, 'Hello Ann'. I turned to see a well-known face from Brighton ice rink days.

'Why, Martin Minchell. What are you doing here?'

'I'm joining you and Joanne's here too.'

They were a nice couple. A former British and world

champion, he was to be one of the stars of our ice show. This was good news. Already I was among friends.

Dad gave me a big hug. 'Keep in touch Ann, and God bless,' He walked away across the concourse and my vision blurred for an instant.

We flew into Tel-Aviv to skate during July and August, the hottest months of the year. At noon we couldn't bear to be out in the sun. It seemed crazy to have an ice show in a place like this.

They laid the ice on the football field, and of course, it kept melting. Then they covered it with a huge canvas tent, made hurriedly by the engineers and backstage helpers. It was like an oven under there. We couldn't start skating for another five days, and then only at 10pm, when the sun had gone down.

Because we had so much time off I did some sightseeing, by myself, quietly, on local buses. Going to Jerusalem a lady pointed out places on the route. 'See, these places are in your Bible,' she said, with pride. 'They are in our holy Scriptures too.'

Jerusalem, with its laden donkeys, trotting over cobbled streets, had a sense of timelessness. Every nation under the sun seemed to be there, making it touristy and commercial. The holy places were jealously guarded but Golgotha, where Jesus died on the cross, had a noisy bus station down below. However, it was peaceful in the Garden of Gethsemane, where eight olive trees, black and gnarled spoke of age and tremendous secrets.

The guardian of the Garden welcomed everyone at the gate. He gave me a leaflet and pointed to a bench in the shade, 'People like to come here and sit down quietly and meditate.' I didn't, because I didn't know at that time how to think very profound thoughts, but something of the peace of that place entered my being. He asked me how long I was going to be in Jerusalem. 'We have communion here on Sundays, if you are free.' I thanked him and made my escape.

After that I organised some sightseeing for the rest of the cast. Every Friday, and Saturday we took a guide and two coaches and toured the places of interest . . . Jerusalem, Bethlehem, Nazareth, Eilat on the Red Sea, the Golan Heights – which was dotted with wrecked Russian tanks, the result of the Six Days War, the year before. We floated in the Dead Sea, reading newspapers. My green rubber plimsolls disintegrated because of the strong minerals in the water. We didn't dare swallow any of it, in case we too disappeared.

With Brigitta, I took a plane to see King Solomon's mines. On the Red Sea in a glass-bottomed boat we studied fishes swimming in the depths, in infinite variety of exotic colours. Then we rode a camel, and felt sea-sick on this ship of the desert.

Most of the cast were staying at the Sheridan Hotel on the beach in Tel-Aviv. I didn't want to waste money on luxurious accommodation, but use it for touring and buying presents. By recommendation, I found a Danish guy who rented rooms in a house on the beach. The door was locked securely but my gold bracelet and Sony radio-alarm disappeared while I was with a family in the next-door house, having lunch. I called the police, who didn't offer much hope of finding the thief. 'Gold can be disposed of quickly.' They thought the man came through the window, which was shuttered and barred.

I had already had one nasty experience with those windows. In the night, disturbed by a noise I woke to see a man at the open shutters. He was trying to remove the iron bars, which I had thought would prevent entry. He was working them loose, when I snatched a knife from an array of weapons on the wall – my Danish landlord was a collector of these – and flung it with all my might at the shape silhouetted against the moonlight. The knife hit the bars and startled him. He ran like a frightened rabbit, and did not come back.

At the show that night a police chief called and asked me

120

if his men could search my room: 'It is a three-day holiday, and I cannot get a warrant to enter the house, and we believe the owner is away. It is a good opportunity. That is all you need to know, but you will be helping Israel.' So that night, plain clothes police met me after the show and took me home in an unmarked jeep. Once inside the room they knocked on the wall which adjoined my host's room. Then they removed the partition, revealing a cache of guns, bullets and a code book, together with Arab clothing, wigs, false beards. A photograph was taken and the wall replaced. They thanked me kindly, warning me not to speak of it, and went, leaving me astonished and shaken. 'I don't want to stay here,' I thought. 'What's going to happen when he comes back?' Then it occurred to me that I could tell him of my robbery and leave him to assume that the thief had also disturbed his hoard.

When I told the Sabra family, next door, they invited me to stay with them. I was grateful, because by then I had a real sense of foreboding about the place. That very night, in fact, the Hungarian girl who rented a room right next to mine was attacked by a man who came through her window.

August, 1968 I remember vividly because we had two weeks' unexpected holiday in England without pay, courtesy of the Russian Air Force. They had bombed Bratislava airport in the brief 'spring' of revolution, on the night we were supposed to be flying in. We had missed the plane from Vienna by half an hour, because of a late departure from Tel Aviv. That could have resulted in disaster for us. We thought sadly of the friends we had made in Prague on our previous visit, and wondered what had happened to them.

In Paris we rehearsed a new show and toured Europe for a while. In January 1969 we flew to Argentina. We were eight days at Luna Park Stadium, Buenos Aires, before flying to Santiago, Chile. The girls of the cast were, as usual, wined and dined, by the promotion people. I had a nice apartment right in the centre of town. The only drawback was the cannon that boomed from the fort, right by us, at midday, to let people know it was time to clock off from work.

I looked for a suitable church, where there was sure to be a lot of social activity going on. An ambassador from America was at the show one night with his family. Daringly I went up afterwards and asked him if he knew of a church I could attend. 'Do you go regularly?' He seemed surprised, and I guessed that he probably thought of showbiz folk as entirely pagan.

Anyway, he took me to an English speaking church. There I met Pastor Jack Graham, who ran the Embassy chapel for the American and British expatriates. The church was surrounded by gardens, and little humming birds darted about the bougainvillaea, sipping nectar and appearing to stand still in the air with tiny quivering wings.

The Grahams invited me to lunch. We got on well and it was only later that I learned that Jack was in pain for most of the time. He hid this well. I had never met such a jolly man.

One afternoon, in the car, while we were driving over the mountains something tugged at my heartstrings. We had come out to sight-see, but through the trees, and vegetation-covered slopes I suddenly caught a glimpse of an everlasting loveliness, that contrasted with my hurried arrivals and departures. I suddenly said, 'Oh I don't know what to do. Something deep down inside tells me that I should stop skating, but how can I? It's the only thing I know how to do well. I used to be happy, but I'm not now. To a lot of people mine would be an exciting life, but I'm just living out of a suitcase.'

'We understand, Ann,' said Jack. 'But it could be that God is speaking to you.' I was puzzled at this. How could God speak to me? He must have thought I knew, because he went on: 'Maybe God is telling you to stop. You'd better obey, or you will not be happy.'

At the same church I met another missionary couple.

The Hunters had adopted three Chilean boys, and they gave me what they called 'Poor man's dish'. I was disappointed when it turned out to be shepherd's pie. Mrs Hunter told me about having no potatoes to make the dish. She said, 'I knelt in the kitchen and I told the Lord that as you were coming I needed some potatoes to make the meal. I asked him to provide. There was a knock at the door and a man asked if I had any material to sell.

'I gave him some and he paid me enough money so I could go down to the market to buy this meal. That's how God answers prayer.'

I thought, 'Phew, I wouldn't want to live that way!'

Sometimes you live to eat your words, like shepherd's pie.

17: Larry

I was sad when the company moved on to Brazil. In the English church in Santiago I had in a short time made a lot of friends who were real, and made me feel as if I belonged somewhere. It was a rare experience.

In Sao Paulo, Brazil, we had two free days while waiting for the equipment to come. In no time I got involved in my usual round of parties and entertainments. One of my contacts was the minister of tourism, who kindly laid on a coach so that I and my friends could look round the city. Outside Sao Paulo we went to a snake farm, and saw one milked for its venom. Not a pretty sight to see those dripping fangs.

Indirectly through this I met a government minister. He arranged for us to stay in a luxurious apartment in Rio de Janeiro, free of charge, with no strings attached.

The other girls always wondered at how I could get people to do things for me, without the exaction of some sort of return. Many of them were running away with the idea that if a man asked them out to dinner they had to sleep with him afterwards. This made me sad, as some of them were only 17 or 18. I didn't want to see them going wrong from the start of their career. I shuddered to think how they would end. 'You don't have to do anything in return,' I told the girls. 'They've got the pleasure of your company. That's payment enough.'

Diane and Joycie came to stay with me. 'Rio is so expensive,' complained Joycie. 'Money runs through my fingers like water.'

'Put it in jewellery,' I advised. It was what I did myself

when I got the chance. And I showed them my emerald bracelet and ring.

The owner of the jewellery store was from Germany. She offered me a discount if I would bring my skating friends. In the end for one or two little favours I did her she gave me a pendant with all the stones you can get in Brazil. 'Holiday on Ice' was engraved on the back. And there was a topaz ring for my Mum.

Before leaving Chile I had been given a message by one of the businessmen in the church: 'Say hello to Terry for me'. I discovered that this Terry was the president of the Rank Organisation in Brazil.

'We must meet for lunch', Terry boomed down the phone in a ripe Australian voice. 'Bring two friends and your bikinis. There's a lovely pool out at the golf club.'

Sitting in a luxurious restaurant by a shimmering blue pool I asked an American behind me to take a movie of our party. This American was, it turned out, the Governor of Pennsylvania, who was busy building up business relations between America and Brazil.

Out of little acorns oak trees grow. As a result of this meeting he and his delegation came to see the show. One of the delegation, Larry, a Jewish millionaire, paid me a lot of attention, and it awakened my interest in him. After a lightning courtship he declared his feelings for me – and it was mutual. This warm glow, like an electric fire switched on inside, was love at last – and it was wonderful. He was so interesting to talk to and listen to . . . so tender in his courtship of me. I had never felt like this before . . . excited and happy when I was with him . . . conscious of the gap when he was away.

He was travelling a lot and so was I but if we were in the same country we would meet and take up our relationship again. It was like having a permanent address for my heart.

In Brazil, in June '69, disaster overtook me two weeks before the end of the show. I was on my toes doing the Hong Kong number with seven others. I didn't fall, didn't do anything but suddenly two bones in my ankle went out and I was in agony.

Derek Boyle was brisk: 'If you don't skate you won't get paid, you won't get your bonus and you won't get your fare paid home.'

'Well, that's a tough assignment,' I said. 'If you want to pay the clinic bills there you are.'

The doctor looked at it and said I wouldn't get better till I stopped skating and rested. No way was I allowed to do that. Every night I skated and every morning I was at the clinic, having treatment. The management paid. Larry got me a car so I could get to the clinic. But each night I went through agonies on my feet. I tried to save myself but only got corrected by the show director. It was pointless to argue . . . I just did the best I could.

At last it was over and we were on our way home for two months' break. At last I could put my feet up and really rest. Except that Larry came to Paris, and I went over to join him. He rented me a gorgeous suite in a hotel right on the Champs Elysee. I could see the Arc de Triomphe in the distance.

I had little money. I was a rich little poor girl, just for a weekend. But when Larry arrived he lavished flowers and gifts on me and anything I wanted I could have.

The one thing I really wanted was to marry him, but I was afraid to bring up the subject, even obliquely, in case I blurted out something tactless, and this rainbow bubble of romance would burst.

How could someone like Larry be single? He was so nice and such fun to be with and he knew how to treat a woman, with tenderness and romance . . . I hoped it would never end . . . this tender relationship. But would it end in marriage? Somehow, deep inside something didn't fit. Still I went on hoping against hope.

The girls in the show were certain I would marry him and thought me a fool for not prodding him into it. For most of them a white wedding was the necessary end to travels, and we frequently discussed the subject. I had never had the dream of walking down the aisle, since Michael's day. I had been too busy chasing what lay round the next corner, or at the end of the rainbow. But now I knew . . . the answer was that nothing lay there. Just another country. Just another beautiful beach. A mountain perhaps. Some experiences good and bad. People . . . but no-one specially who belonged to me, except Larry. And did he belong to me, really?

And if we did marry, what then? Would he settle down? Wouldn't I be just as bored with his form of travel . . . always on the go, staying in the best hotels but never at home?

During those two months in Portslade I gave shows of the films I had taken abroad to all my friends and relations. I told my first guests that I had brought home real Brazilian coffee. My sister went out to the kitchen to make it, and found it at the bean stage. Exasperated, and unable to find a grinder, she put the beans in a frying pan and barred everyone from the kitchen.

Shortly a delicious aroma of Brazilian coffee wafted out to our nostrils. Expectantly we all drank deeply of the liquid she served. 'M-m-m,' was the verdict, 'Smashing coffee, Ann.'

Only after they had gone did my laughing sister confess that it had been Maxwell House the guests had drunk. 'You could have at least given me ground coffee to start with,' she said.

During the two months I signed up with a temporary agency and drew on my early training in shorthand and typing to earn a bit of money. Mother was managing our furniture shop in Hove and dashing home at lunch times. Dad was now a director of Greenfields, the furniture removers.

Work at the bank was very stuffy, and I hated it. But a high official commented on my appearance, and that made me feel better. Jeans were the office rig at that time while I dressed with formal style. My wardrobe was full of lovely clothes, which I had gathered round the world.

The two months were up and I should have returned to the show in Europe, but I didn't want to. I was so hurt by the way I had been treated in Brazil, that the whole idea stuck in my throat.

'I won't be coming back,' I told some of the girls when I met them unexpectedly at the Strand Palace in London. Larry and I were there seeing the show, 'Sweet Charity'. Several of them expressed surprise.

But I had to earn a living and skating promised more money than typing. In the end I rang Gerald Palmer in London and asked him for a job.

'Pleased to hear from you Ann. I'll give you understudy money but I'm not sure what you'll be doing yet.'

He told me he was going to South Africa to see if he could put on a non-segregated show. 'I'll put you in that if it comes off.'

I landed a part in 'Queen of Hearts on Ice' at Wembley stadium. One night Morris Chalfen, looking for talent, was in the audience. He came back stage: 'Where's that Terry?' he bawled affectionately, waving an aromatic cigar.

'Come back to "Holiday on Ice" he boomed. 'I need you in the Far East. I also need you in South America. You have a choice. Where do you want to go?'

'If you would like to pay me an American salary, instead of an English one, I'll go to South America,' I said.

I'll think about it,' he replied, cautiously.

Thirty six hours after the show finished in England I was on my way to Montevideo, Uruguay.

The cast were complete strangers to me, and the show was new. However, Magda, the Polish head girl, and I started rehearsals right away and I told her I would be in the show that night. I had been on half salary enough times to know I had better learn quickly. 'I don't believe you,' said Magda. 'No one can learn that fast.'

Right enough I took my place in the line-up for 'Thoroughly Modern Millie', dressed in a short, beaded and sequinned red, black and white dress and hat. I loved it. I can still do the steps.

I zipped myself out of that and into 'Scheherazade' – chiffon trousers and sequinned top with a bare midriff. We wove in and out among the smoke-pots, holding the train of a girl who was carried by two men, while doing the splits in the air. It sounds impossible, but she managed it without a wince.

This was the tour when I began to feel really ill. Dizziness hit me at odd times – bending down to do up my laces, coming out of a pirouette. There was a tremendous pressure at the back of my neck, and I wondered how I would get through. Our apartments were eight miles out of town and we got there by taxi. It was awkward because there was a curfew, and shows had to finish early, to get everyone off the streets. The Tuparmaros had kidnapped the British ambassador just before we arrived. It created a queer, nervy atmosphere in the show.

Out on a date with a ship's captain I met the Tuparmaros at the point of a gun. They pushed in to the office where we were having coffee, raked us with eyes as steely as their rifle muzzles, and went out without a word.

'Looking for someone,' said the captain, suddenly white under his tan. 'I'm glad you were here, or it might have been curtains for me.'

I was grateful when the tour drew to a close, but trouble loomed. When I came off the ice from a jazz number on the last night I ran into a posse of police backstage, with rifles cocked.

'Ann they want you,' said the manager wearing a baffled expression. 'They say you haven't paid your rent bill.'

'There were four people in our apartment and we *all* paid.' I said it with some heat.

We discovered then the folly of not getting receipts. The police showed that they intended to march me into the van. 'I'll come with you Ann, and my boy friend. He

129

speaks the language.' That was Carol – the only room-mate to stand by me. Was I grateful!

At the police station I remembered my rights and asked to be allowed one phone call. Quickly I got through to a friend, the son of an ambassador, who was waiting for me to join him at the bar of the Sheridan Hotel. He came right over, like a gentleman.

Then he bargained with them for my freedom, offering to remain and pay the bill, if I could be let go to catch the plane out of the country. It took hours of patient negotiation, but in the end he won. So while I sped off to Argentina, he was locked into a cell, where, I later heard, he remained for three days, in spite of having paid the bill again.

When I hear of terrible things happening in South America now, I am not surprised. Human rights seem to have little meaning there. Money is the only thing that talks, usually.

18: Final Curtain

The show dropped anchor in Buenos Aires for a month, and I went to the English hospital every day for treatment, as my back was playing up.

In Barranquila, Colombia, the customs at the airport seized our ice-machine because we would not pay the sum they asked for its release. 'Chance would be a fine thing,' said the ice engineers. 'We could buy two more ice-machines with that. We can't afford that kind of money.' And we did not skate for a week, which of course hit us pretty hard.

The management were getting desperate. 'Ann, haven't you any ideas?' Jose the manager asked. 'Yes, I've got an idea,' I said. And under my breath I added, 'But you won't like it.'

So I asked the manager of the hotel to arrange a press conference. Later that day a crowd of reporters from the main newspapers assembled in the lounge. Telling them about the seizure of the ice-making machine I said, 'We are poor ice skaters, with no money and we want to skate for your people. Would you please publish this so that our ice-machine can be released?'

'Is it true that you only get seven dollars a day?'

'It's true,' I said. 'When we don't work we don't get paid our full salary. We can't eat properly, because it goes in hotel bills.'

The reporters did their stuff and the ice machine was freed soon after.

Through seeing my picture in the papers, another Larry came into my life. This one was the director of a tin plant

131

in Bogota. He found out where I was staying and called me.

Our romance grew, even though I had the other Larry in the background. But I had not heard from him for more than a year – and here was a flesh and blood Larry who was more than ready to take his place. 'I am trying to get a divorce,' he told me. 'My wife has gone back to Ireland with my son and our marriage is over. I love you.'

I believed him. It was good to hear words of love when I was so lonely and travelling thousands of miles from home. He was a lot of fun, generous and crazy like I was. Once he careered on to a green in his sports car, while a golf tournament was in progress, to pick up my girl friend who had collapsed. Swooping her up, he got away through the crowd, before anyone could stop him.

Larry went back to Ireland to settle up his affairs. At the airport he kissed me and told me to get ready to leave the show. 'I'll see you at Christmas. We'll fly down to Mexico, where I'll be working.'

He sounded so confident. At last I could settle down somewhere, and have a home of my home. The dreams expanded to fill my lonely nights.

My manager arranged for a girl in the Far East tour to fly in and take my place. He bought me my ticket. I had a letter from Morris Chalfen saying, 'I am so happy for you', everything was falling neatly into place.

I boarded the aircraft for our next stop, Quito, Ecuador, in a rosy glow of happiness. There were three of us from the show planning to be married, Jean Sweetman, Scotty and I, and we sat together. Jean Sweetman's fiancé, Victor, was on board too. A fighter pilot who had survived the second world war, he was a hero to the cast. It didn't seem to matter that he was years older than Jean.

We were just chatting pleasantly when, without warning, the bottom dropped out of the sky and we were going straight down, accelerating fast. The luggage jumped off the racks and fell on us. There were screams of anguish and terror. We were going to crash! We waited in deadly fear for the impact that would blot out everything. 'Sit down!' shouted Victor to the hysterical passengers. 'You are unbalancing the aircraft.'

Suddenly I knew, with a calm certainty that I was not going to die. I hadn't met God yet. With startling clarity I saw this had been my life's quest. I heard myself shouting above the cries of the other passengers: 'Sit down. We are not going to crash. We are going to live. Just start praying.'

At that moment the engines gunned and the pilot somehow pulled the plane's nose out of the dive, and we levelled out. Over the intercom came his strained voice, 'The engine stalled. We fell thousands of feet, but we are all right now.'

There was a general sigh of relief as we scrambled back into our seats and hoisted the luggage to the racks.

Victor wiped his brow, 'I really thought we were goners then,' he said, putting his arms around Jean and hugging her tight.

It was as well that day that we could not see what the future held. Within three years, Jean, married to her Victor, died of cancer. Victor, married a second time disappeared in his plane over the Venezuelan mountains. And the cards that life dealt me were not what I expected.

In Guayaquil, Ecuador, a few nights later, I had a dream. I was receiving a telegram. I held the crisp white paper in my hand and read, 'Wedding off. Don't leave show. Reconciled with Maeve. Letter awaiting you in Savoy Hotel, Lima, Peru, Larry.' I woke with tears running down my face, and a terrible sense of foreboding. Scotty had heard me cry out and she was now awake too. 'What's wrong, Ann?' she asked.

I told her my dream. 'I know it's going to come true,' I sobbed.

Practical Scotty thought of a quick remedy. 'Come on, let's get dressed and go shopping.'

For once, it didn't tempt me, but I went with her. Walking along, talking and not minding where I was going

I didn't notice the drain hole in front of me till I fell in, waist deep. Then I overbalanced into the road, inches from some onward roaring car wheels.

With a terrible screeching of tyres the car came to a halt and an ashen-faced driver rushed to my rescue. 'I think I've broken my ankle,' I sobbed. It was swelling up like a balloon. How was I going to skate?

The driver, who spoke English, took us to a clinic. There doctors looked at the ankle, decided it was badly sprained, and wanted to plaster it. I refused. If they did that I would be out of work and out of pay. It seemed an impossibility, but somehow I had to get on the ice that night. With promises to return for treatment I asked Scotty to call a taxi and we got back to the hotel in time to get ready.

I knew what I had to do . . . fake it. I managed to get into the dressing room without being seen to limp. Then, just before my number I took off the bandages, squeezed my foot into its skating boot, pulled on my clown trousers and somehow got on the ice. Then I simply and spectacularly fell, spreadeagled on the ice. It was a most magnificent accident. I was picked up, carted to the dressing room and my damaged ankle drew satisfactory cries of sympathy.

The result was that I returned to the clinic in style, my treatment was paid for, and I was given half a week's salary for the next two weeks. I'd got away with murder. Scotty thought it was a great idea to fleece the management.

'Serves them right for being such skinflints,' she said, approvingly.

That was nothing, however, to the pain I suffered next morning when a telegram was handed to me. Just as in my dream I held the crisp white paper in my hand and read, 'Wedding off. Don't leave show. Reconciled with Maeve. Letter awaiting you in Savoy Hotel, Lima, Peru. Larry.'

The cast reacted to this news as family would have done. The girls gathered round and acted as if they hurt too. They got their boy-friends to carry me out to restaurants, so I wouldn't brood alone. The men in the show phoned Morris Chalfen for me.

'Terry, you stay with the show,' he said gruffly, as if he had tears in his eyes. 'I know what it is to lose someone precious. The best thing is work. You don't want to go to England now, do you?'

'No I don't,' I said, weeping. I could just hear my family saying, 'Poor Ann.' I didn't want their pity just then.

So in the words of one of the numbers to which I skated, it was 'On with the motley, the paint and the powder. . . .' The show couldn't stop, for a sprained ankle or a broken heart.

Morris made arrangements for me to stay with the cast while we transferred ourselves by boat to Antofagasta, in Chile. I blessed him for his kindness.

On a stopover in Lima, Peru, I received Larry's letter explaining everything.

'She tried to commit suicide, because she loved me so much, and couldn't bear the thought of my marrying anyone else. The hospital managed to bring her round. But it's been a shock to me and my family. I feel I must make the most of my marriage for her sake. She is a Catholic and doesn't believe in divorce.'

It went on for several pages. Eventually I realised that what he really wanted was to stay married to Maeve, but to keep in touch with me. The idea chilled me. He wanted to have his cake and eat it. At that moment I thought of Maeve more than myself. He had to be faithful to her, having made his decision. I plucked up the strength to write back:

'As you have made the decision to make the most of your marriage, then you need to utterly cut yourself off from hearing from me again.'

So ended another painful episode in my life. Would I ever be happy? Could I ever trust men again? In that place where girls normally keep an imaginary snapshot of themselves walking down the aisle in white there was nothing . . . just a blank.

It left a nasty taste in everyone's mouth, because Larry had been universally popular with the cast.

'I'm not selling my skating boots in case that happens to me,' said Jean. Show people are very superstitious and a feeling of bad luck brewing crept over me.

Six months later, in Rio de Janeiro, Brazil, walking into the Maracanazino football stadium, I collapsed. One minute I was fine . . . the next I was flat on the concrete floor.

My back hurt dreadfully. I couldn't move. The football stadium doctor was called to look at me. A brief examination revealed nothing, so an appointment was made for me to have an x-ray next day. While the performance went on I lay in the dressing room in terrible pain, unable to walk.

The doctor thought it was my bones and he put me in traction. That did not help at all. The same thing happened again. And again. It was as if a hand was pushing me down, down, till I lay flat on the ground. I really began to be afraid that it might be some evil power. I had met a voodoo priestess once, and I wondered if evil was contagious, like measles. Or did someone wish me hurt?

Then an English friend introduced me to her doctor, a back specialist. He took loads of x-rays, and came up with the answer that my whole constitution was crying out for rest.

'How soon can you leave the show?' he asked, seriously.

I told him I was halfway through my contract, and couldn't leave. I hadn't the money.

People thought I was putting this on . . . that my wealthy Jewish boy-friend was back and I wanted time off to see him. 'Is Larry back in town, Ann?'

I wished it had been true. I didn't know where Larry was. But no one would believe me. I stayed off work for five days and during that time I really prayed to God.

'God help me. I'm five thousand miles away from home, and I don't know what to do.'

136

It was as if a harsh voice spoke, jeeringly, 'God can't hear you. There's too much sin in your life.'

I looked around the room. The voice was so real. But there was no one. I carried on praying.

Then in front of my eyes rose up all the things I had ever done wrong, that God would be displeased with. The people I had hurt. Michael. Erkhardt. My family. I had been self-centred, proud.

I stood accused before the bar of God's supreme justice. My guilt was clear. And I had no defence, no excuse. I knew I had to get right with God. How could I do that?

For most of this time I was alone . . . the others were either at the show or out sunning themselves on the beach. But one day there was a knock on the door and in walked Rudi. He was the accountant, a cheerful Dutchman. He asked if I had heard the good news.

'The first five girls and seven boys who go to the office tomorrow morning can have their bonus, and their fare paid home.'

No, I hadn't heard, but I wanted it very badly. 'How am I going to get there?' I asked in distress. The office was at the Copacabana Hotel, in Rio.

I knew that everyone would want out. All except me had been on tour for two years. Rudi smiled. 'It's all right Ann, I've put you on this list.' I could have hugged him.

I was so filled with joy and relief that I forgot about my back and got up to make him a cup of tea. But it made no difference. No more skating for Ann Terry. The curtain had finally rung down!

19: Home

In July, 1971 I arrived in New York and checked in at a hotel in 45th Street. There, a friend I had made in Sioux City tried to get me a job so that I could stay. But I had to have a green card.

I got work for two weeks with a skating circus in Newhaven, Connecticut, but I couldn't take the permanency they offered without a work permit.

My sister, who was in Massachusetts, married to an American, indirectly found me a job selling hand-carved doors. If she had become an American citizen I could have got a permit, but that fell through.

I found another job, in Arizona, with Snelling & Snelling, the largest employment agency in the US. I even took a short management course with them, in case the permit came through. Then the prize was offered to me . . . becoming director of an ice rink, back in Massachusetts. I had never been so spoiled for choice but so helpless. It was especially galling as there was a lot of unemployment around, and firms usually gave jobs to the locals first.

The owner of the ice rink paid for a lawyer to fight the immigration regulations, and here Senator Edward Kennedy became involved with my case. Ted, as he was called by everyone, was often asked to help people trying to settle in the States. But even he couldn't soften the immigration authorities.

The crunch came when I was told to go by two burly investigating officers who confronted me in Sudbury,

Massachusetts, where I was staying, taking care of a friend's kids for a while.

'We can't renew your visitor's visa. You've made it plain you want to stay permanently. You'll have to go back to England and try from there. You'll have to leave by October.'

No sooner had they gone than the phone went. Senator Kennedy's secretary was on the line: 'Ted says to tell you that we're fighting something more powerful here than the US State Department.'

'Do you mean God?' I asked.

'Yes,' she said. End of conversation.

Later that day the pastor of the local Episcopalian church I had been attending came to see how my back was. It had started playing me up at the very mention of the word 'skating'.

'You shouldn't be here,' he said. 'Not in Sudbury, not in Massachusetts, not in the USA. You should go back to England. God will meet you there.'

When the dust settled and I had time to think this through I felt really riled. What business was it of God's where I lived? Why did I have to go back to England? Now that it faced me in reality I couldn't bear the thought of the claustrophobic society I had known in Portslade. Also I had spent two thousand pounds trying to stay in America. I shook my fist in the air at God. 'You had better take care of me, God. I don't want to go back to that country. It means nothing to me.'

On October 13th I arrived in Southampton and was met by my Dad.

Back in my own room in Trafalgar Road I found thirty parcels I had sent to myself from Japan. My Hong Kong chest was full of the haul from thirteen years of globe-trotting. Dad fixed the plug on my shell lamp from the Philippines and I stood carved figurines on a handy shelf, laid beside my bed the sheepskin rug, donated by Australia to my Aladdin's treasure cave, and wondered what to do with stacks of books from everywhere. It was like Christmas round the world and I sat amongst it all and wondered what I was going to do next.

Mum had an idea that I ought to go into acting in movies. She was becoming quite successful herself in a small way. I learned that my sister Pat had sent a photograph of her to a film studio and to everyone's surprise she got parts in TV commercials – pulling the bottom tin from the pile in supermarkets, and making the stack fall, and all that sort of thing. She even got a bit part in 'Oh What a Lovely War!'

I couldn't quite work up the enthusiasm wanted of me, until the studio rang and asked if she had any daughters. They wanted us for a factory scene, with the shift coming out.

This led on to my being a stand-in for Gayle Hunnicutt. I was chosen because I was dark, slim and the right height. But my job description took on a very literal meaning, when I was asked to stand in the rain for her. Firemen would hose me to simulate a downpour as the cameras took their shots. I thought this was a miserable idea and refused it.

I appeared next in the film of Joe Orton's 'Loot'. This meant sitting at a cafe table on Brighton racecourse, pretending to be in France. Some horses charged through the 'cafe' and we got danger money for it. It came to about thirty pounds, which was quite a lot for one day's work.

This however was no permanent solution and anyway I found it boring to be hanging around all day, waiting for the little bit I had to do, in any kind of weather.

In the end, after making several different moves I settled on working for a big corporation. American Express wanted secretaries? Right then, a secretary I would be till something better turned up.

My boss, David Newman was a super chap, full of good humour, which kept me going through the times when I felt blue. The adjustments to be made in settling into office work were enormous . . . something that not many people around me could have understood.

To rise every morning at six o'clock and get from Portslade to Burgess Hill by nine o'clock was very difficult after my timetable as a skater. Then I had been free all day, and only had to work in a limited number of hours at night, apart from rehearsals, though the work was very hard and concentrated. Here I had to work all day, and come home exhausted at night. When the sun shone I wanted to be out walking or swimming or sightseeing, or meeting people. Instead I was trapped in an office, at other people's beck and call.

Aunt Win couldn't understand why I hadn't thought of this. 'Surely you knew before you took this job that it would be like this?' she queried, looking exasperated. Mum said, 'You are making us all unhappy. Why don't you go back into show business?'

I couldn't explain that I had been brought to England against my will, and that skating was not for me. I couldn't understand it myself.

Christmas Eve arrived with me in a very low state. I had no desire to celebrate. But I did go to a carol service at St Andrews where I had once been a Sunday School teacher. Then carol services were crammed. But this one was attended by six people. We were all huddled near the back while the minister stood way out in front and shouted to us over a great gulf. The carols, readings and prayers dragged on for an hour, while the six of us made our feeble responses at the back, and I for one prayed for it to end.

Suddenly, I felt the most tremendous thirst, as if I had eaten loads of salt. I had a distinct impression that it was not water that would quench my thirst. What ran through my mind were the words, 'I want to know God'. It was as if the thirst came from deep down.

When the service was over I dashed out without waiting to speak to anyone and ran home. Upstairs on the second floor I found my trunk in the box room and dug out my travel-stained green Bible. I knelt on the floor, wanting to read it but not knowing where to look. The Bible slid to the floor, and opened at a page, closed and reopened. Picking it up, I looked at the page and the fine print suddenly came out at me. The words said this: 'He that hungers and thirsts after righteousness shall be filled'. I saw that it was from Matthew 5. My eye travelled down the page and another sentence expanded like a sign: 'You are the salt of the earth.'

I sat there bemused. 'This is talking about me,' I said aloud. 'I feel as if I've eaten loads of salt. I am thirsty to know God. What shall I do now?'

A voice spoke to me audibly in the silence of the room. 'It's midnight. Go to bed.'

All that night I tossed and turned, trying to work out what it all meant. At six o'clock I was up and dressed and down in the kitchen, making a cup of tea. Mother came in to put the turkey in the oven and exclaimed, 'What are you doing up so early?'

'I couldn't sleep. I'm going out.'

'Sit down and I'll make you some breakfast. It's too early to go out.'

At nine o'clock I put on my coat, not knowing where I was going, when I felt a hand pushing me in the back, out through the kitchen, through the lounge, out of the back door. Round by the conservatory I went under the most extraordinary guiding pressure. I wasn't afraid, just full of expectancy. Down the road I went, and into a small church I had never visited before, the Southern Cross Free Evangelical.

Then the pressure lifted. I thought, 'I've got a choice now.' I stood and looked at the door and half decided to go, then turned back and sat down. 'If this hand has bothered to guide me here there must be a reason,' I thought to myself.

A voice spoke my name. 'Ann, welcome to God's family'. A woman was standing beside me. She answered

142

my unspoken question. 'I live next door to your Nan Hornsby. I've seen your skating photographs.'

Suddenly I noticed the people around me. There was something different about them. They looked full of peace and the most exquisite joy. The songs they were singing were unfamiliar to me. Not dreary hymns but joyful, happy songs about God. I fumbled in my hymn book but she leaned over and closed it and said, 'You won't find them there. They are from the Bible.'

I looked at her, like a wondering child, and asked, 'What is it that you have got and they have got and I haven't?'

She replied, 'We know the Lord Jesus Christ. Don't you?'

The service was about to commence so we left it there. The whole service was different to anything I had met before, especially the talk given by the minister.

I don't remember now what he said but while he was talking it was as if the meaning was being interpreted to me. I saw that the greatest gift I could ever receive was Jesus Christ as my Saviour. I saw that he didn't just die on the cross for people in that generation but for all people everywhere in all times who would receive him as Saviour.

If I expected this to be followed up I was disappointed. 'Your speech really spoke to me,' I told the pastor. To which he replied, 'That's good. You live over the road. Well, we'll see you again then.'

I felt quite let down, abandoned at the threshold of something very important. I went home, almost in despair. There followed three months of darkness and depression. I was the most miserable person around.

In February, an old skating friend, Jenny Reygate, asked me to go skiing in Austria. That should have made me happy, but it didn't. I was miserable.

It was a funny experience altogether – the reverse of skating, where you leaned inwards to stop. There you leaned outwards. My skis which turned out to be for racing raced off with me, out of control. The instructors were for ever chasing after me while I squealed desperately, 'Achtung! Achtung!' Usually it ended with me being scooped out of a snowdrift by a really handsome instructor. It was a good way to meet some nice men, but it didn't do a lot for my skiing.

After a lovely holiday I came home, but the depression hadn't lifted. It followed me around like a huge black cloud.

My father's sickness didn't help. I was very fond of my Dad and I felt sure there was something really wrong. There was, though the full extent was not revealed till later in the year.

That was a black year. Dad was made bankrupt through no fault of his own. We had to move out of our house and into a smaller one. Two days after that move, Dad was rushed into hospital with a heart condition. In the middle of all this blackness I had an unresolved problem. What to do with the knowledge I had been given about Jesus Christ. How could I get to know him? There were people across the road who knew him. My mother suggested that I go to the doctor, because I wasn't sleeping at night. I did and he put me on tranquillisers. 'What is my life?' I thought. 'I've been stopped from skating. Brought back to England. Made to be a second-class secretary, in a boring office. What is my life for?'

One Wednesday I came back from work at six o'clock, and while Mother was taking my dinner from the oven I rushed across the road to the manse and burst into tears on the doorstep. 'God's stopped talking to me. I'm so lonely.' And I poured out the whole story. The minister was really kind. He listened and then said. 'God is speaking to you and that's why you are here. We have been waiting for you.'

It turned out that the whole church had been praying for me. 'We know something happened to you on Christmas Day.'

He went on talking using a lot of foreign terminology,

about praying, and studying the word of God. But however mystifying the language I understood this much – that people here really cared, and that this was where I was meant to be.

I began to go to that church every Sunday, and gradually began to feel more settled.

20: The Ice Breaks

One day, in April, when the flowers were springing and the birds singing, Larry, my American-Jewish boyfriend, came back into my life. His letter dropped on me, like a bomb. He wrote:

'I know I haven't been in touch for quite a while but do you think we could have a groovy relationship? Could I see you? I am coming through London on a business trip and staying at the Savoy Hotel in London. Could you book yourself a room there?'

I was knocked for six . . . excited would be too mild a word. But I didn't jump to the invitation as the old Ann would have done. I knew now he was married. There could be no other explanation for why he had stayed out of my life so long. That time in Paris . . . the love we had known was so real and had made such an impact on my life, and he had been such a lot of fun, that to be cut off like that had been like dying.

No, too much had changed in me to expect me to pick up where we left off as though nothing had happened. I had proved I could do without him. Furthermore what he wanted of me was wrong. So I wrote back:

'It would be lovely to see you to catch up on your news, but I'm not so sure about the groovy relationship. Send me a telegram to say when to come. But I'd prefer you to book me a room.'

I said that because I didn't want to be left stranded in an expensive room in a London hotel, if he decided not to come.

So we met, after four years. He had got fatter, balder

and he suffered with asthma, but the old charm was there. He was still kind and warm, and very, very smart, with expensive, tailor-made lightweight suit and silk tie.

He had booked me, not just a room but a whole suite at the Savoy, on the same floor as his, and I occupied it joyfully for three nights, lapping up the luxury after being deprived for so long. We had plenty of time to catch up with news.

He showed me photographs of his family. 'There was a time Ann when I would have travelled anywhere in the world to have the excuse of seeing you and being with you, but then disaster struck. I nearly went bankrupt and needed to borrow several million dollars. My wife became very ill and we nearly lost her. My eldest son had a car accident. Everything happened at once and everything was against me. I had to stick with them all. Now I am wealthier than I have ever been, but I've changed through this ordeal. The pressure has caused me to have asthma, but I've realised how much my family means to me. I wanted to see you and tell you this personally.'

'I'm grateful you did,' I said. 'But I've changed too.' And I told him how I had been forced to leave skating, and of the answers I was getting in my search for God and of the adjustments I had had to make back in the ordinary world. I told him about Irish Larry, and how I broke my heart over that experience.

He took my hand. 'I'm sorry you've had all this, but knowing you, you'll make things happen and pull out of it.'

Monday morning I was chauffeur-driven to American Express. Cinders had come back from the ball. She would never meet this Prince Charming again.

Judith from the church became a close friend about this time. 'Come round any time,' she said. And I took her up on it.

She was a schoolteacher and seemed quite clever. I hadn't managed to get one O-level and had an outsize inferiority complex about it. I argued with her about the

147

truth of the Bible, the need for Christ to die for my sins, and how did one get born again? Some of her answers didn't make sense, but they must have been going in all the same because one night at home, the need to speak to God myself became urgent.

I knelt down in my bedroom and I prayed, 'God, I've been speaking to you for years. I know you. But I don't know your Son Jesus. In the Bible it says that your Son died on the cross for me. If I ask him into my life I know he will take over my life. So God, I am asking Jesus to come into my life tonight. I believe the plan you have for my life is greater than anything I can do for myself. Amen.

Then I added quickly, feeling it to be necessary: 'PS. I believe by faith that you have come in. Please, will you make up for all the years I've wasted.'

I didn't feel any different. I just got into bed and went to sleep, at peace. But the following morning was different altogether. I woke up with such joy in my heart that I began to sing. Out came all the choruses I had heard at Southern Cross. I had never consciously learned them. Anyway, my memory gave me trouble since the car crash in Italy nine years earlier. Now that had been mended, and my appreciation of the world had changed too – I saw with new eyes. The colours in our garden were clean and clear and soft. Sounds I heard charmed me – birdsong was sweet, and brought tears to my eyes. Like a child I skipped everywhere.

Judith took me to the Scripture Union book shop in Brighton, where I bought a leather-bound Revised Standard version of the Bible. The words fell like prisms into my mind. Many-sided in meaning, they brought new depths of understanding about life and God. This book was more than a book – it was a love letter from God, telling me how much he loved me, first in creating me, then in keeping me safe all the years of travelling round the world, then in bringing me to know Jesus right here at my own front door. 'And this is eternal life, that they know thee the only true God, and Jesus Christ whom thou hast sent,' said the book. (John 17. 3) I realised that eternal life was mine now.

People saw I had changed. My Dad said, 'What's up, Ann? You're like a two-year old.'

'I've given my heart to the Lord Jesus, and now I feel so happy.'

Mother cut me off sharply. 'Don't talk to us about God.'

So I didn't then, but I was talking about him to everyone else – at work, in the buses, when I was eating my sandwiches on the seat in the Martlets. And people stopped swearing when I was around.

My first public testimony was two weeks later at the sea front at the bottom of Grand Avenue, by Queen Victoria's statue. I spoke to the passers-by and holidaymakers, telling them what had happened to me, as a result of going round the world and running out of steam, before I met Jesus.

The old queen looked severe at this self-revelation. The holidaymakers looked interested. I felt nervous, because it was a responsibility to talk about Jesus under these circumstances. But I found I had a gift of evangelising when I went with the church, door to door, singing carols. I was left behind quite often, as I was invited in to share with the people in the houses what Jesus meant to me.

Not long after this I went with the church to some Fountain Trust meetings at Westminister Central Hall, and there I came into an understanding of just what Jesus did for me on the cross, when he died for my sins. I realised also that many of the things I had been involved with, such as palmistry, fortune-telling, the ouija board and the like were an abomination to God, (as seen in Deuteronomy 18. 10-13).

I saw that what had appeared like a bit of fun at the time, was actually a bondage put on me by Satan to hinder my spiritual growth. I needed to be set free from all his

149

abominable works. Michael Harper and another minister prayed for me, and I felt a warm glow and I knew I was free from that part of my past.

The following Easter I went to a holiday conference at Watcombe House, Dorset, wanting all that God had to give me. I came away knowing that he was building me into the Body of Christ, which is his Church. From that time on I had intimations that he was also preparing me for a new work.

That September I went to Filey. David Watson was giving the Bible studies, and they fell like refreshing water on my spirit. At the end of the week, one of the main speakers, Alan Redpath, got everyone to stand who wanted to serve the Lord. I stood among the crowd, but no lightning flash fell to direct my path.

But I had a piece of advice from David Watson. 'Go home and tell your pastor how you are feeling about becoming an evangelist,' said that lovely man of God. On my mind was a piece of land I owned in Deltona, Florida, which I felt I had to give away on God's instructions. I didn't know to whom, and I wasn't in Florida. But in the end I was shown that I should give it to a Christian organisation, so I did. It was just another weight, tying me to this world. I had had too much of this world.

On my return home I talked with my pastor, Ken Blackwell, and as we prayed together about my commitment, Youth With a Mission School of Evangelism came strongly to mind.

Four months later, in January 1975, I was there, at the school in Ifield Hall, Crawley, studying the Bible for three months.

At Easter thirty-six of us students, left for Europe, to put into practice all we had learned. More than three hundred pounds had come, without any advertising of my need, also a sleeping bag, a lilo, movie films, some jeans and longer dresses – so many of mine were minis and unsuitable for Moslem countries in which we would be travelling.

By the time all expenses were taken care of I had twenty pounds in my pocket to last me three months, which would involve travel through many of the countries of Europe. Let me list them: France, Germany, Austria, Italy, Greece, Turkey, Rhodes, Cyprus, Israel, Rumania, Bulgaria, Russia, Yugoslavia and back to Holland.

Two things amazed me . . . one, that God could provide for all my needs. I even returned with four pounds. Two, that I was working over the ground I had travelled as a skater with 'Holiday on Ice', and even had the golden opportunity of talking about Christ to two people from that past life – Ivan and Oleg, the Russian scientists.

Eleven years had gone by and yet they were just as warm and friendly, but I noticed the strain on their faces. They came individually. Ivan took a New Testament to read, and the next day invited us to his home to meet his wife.

'I've been up all night, reading this book,' he said, sounding excited. 'Now what do I do? Where do I go to church?'

I left him to my friends, who knew the Bible better than I did, while I spoke to his wife. Before I left, on the phone he said, 'Thank you Ann for coming back and giving me hope for a change of life.'

He sounded choked with sadness. I felt frustrated that I could not stay longer, or help him more. I just had to leave him in God's hands. But I prayed for him and for Oleg, and still do. There are many behind the Iron Curtain who have faith and cannot express it openly, without incurring persecution.

Israel I saw with new eyes, not just as a tourist, this time. The land came alive and matched the book. In the Garden of Gethsemane I met Colonel Ord Dobbie, and told him of my previous visit and the change in the way I saw this place, now I had been born again. 'I am very happy for you,' he said.

Our group stayed at a hostel at Tiberias on the shore of the Sea of Galilee, and I was up at four o'clock as the sun rose in crimson splendour, and lit a path for me, as I sat on a rock in the calm sea, meditating. I was back in Bible times, where Jesus walked . . . and I was content.

* * *

I could go on for ever. Life had not stood still for me since then . . . it never does for the servant of the Lord. I am still travelling on, learning more each day of his perfect will for my life.

Isaiah 43. 1, 2 seems a fair commentary on all that has happened to me, even if it doesn't mention ice:

> 'Fear not, for I have redeemed you; I have called you by name, you are mine. When you pass through the waters, I will be with you; and through the rivers, they shall not overwhelm you; when you walk through fire you shalt not be burned, and the flame shall not consume you. For I am the Lord your God . . . your Saviour.'

21: Afterwords

'You haven't changed, Ann. After all these years you are still the same. The speaker was Scotty, and we were sitting together in her new home in Weston-super-Mare, early in January, 1985, at our first meeting for fifteen years. Her husband Pete, who was in electronics, and their six-year-old son Steve, were also enjoying the reunion.

'Do you remember that time in Guayacil, Ecuador, Ann?' The photograph Scotty handed me showed us as two leggy girls in mini-skirts, standing in a foreign street, by a harbour, with ships; in the background, a hotel. Memories came flooding back. That was when I fell down the drain hole in the main street, and deceived the company into thinking I had hurt myself on the ice, so getting half pay while convalescing.

Peter broke into my thoughts: 'Wasn't that where you faked the accident, Ann?'

That incident, passed over so lightly then, had returned to trouble me when I joined YWAM. Don Stevens, director of the Lausanne school had been telling us about an incident in his own life when he had had to get something out in the open he would much rather have kept hidden. He explained that God is a God of light, and in him is no darkness at all.

Suddenly, like blinding daylight it had hit me . . . the Ecuador incident, when I had cheated the company. God spoke to my heart and said, 'You must write to Morris Chalfen and ask him to forgive you, and be willing to pay back any money owing.'

Scared, I wrote the letter, and waited in suspense for a reply. It came swiftly.

'What was in it?' Scotty's eyes were wide with surprise as I related this story. 'I could never do that!'

'He said he was pleased to hear from me, and by my letter I had made restitution. He had always regarded me as an honest person and I owed him nothing. He wished me every success and happiness in the new life I had found, and good luck in becoming a missionary.'

'Did you have to do that?' said Scotty.

I said. 'Yes, what I did was wrong. I wouldn't have had any peace if I hadn't done it.'

That had been only one of the messy pieces of the past I had had to sort out when I became a believing Christian.

'You were always up to something,' said Scotty, shaking her head in disbelief, and the conversation moved on. Time flew by. When I left at one o'clock in the morning, I had to promise to see them again. I went away very thoughtful.

Scotty had got out of show-business and found happiness with her Peter. What did I bring away from all those years?

Certainly I treasured friendships with people like Scotty . . . people whom I could trust. Shirley-Marie was another, and Monica. I learned something about human nature during those years, which has stood me in good stead. I am nobody's pushover now.

I certainly achieved my early ambitions, having the opportunity to travel and see the world, doing what I loved and being paid for it. But, during those years I grew up and became a different person. By the end of fifteen years of world travel I had outgrown the chorus line, and the whole life. It emptied as I went, and I had nothing to show for it. By about the third time round the world it was time to get off the merry-go-round . . . and when I wouldn't get off on my own volition, God engineered my circumstances, so that I would stop.

Why did God take so much trouble over me? He was

trying to get my attention right back in childhood, from the age of three, when I can remember standing by the back door and saying aloud, 'What am I doing here?'

All the influences that played on me from Nanny Terry, from Sunday School and church, and from contact with Christians through my skating career, led me in the end to one inescapable conclusion . . . that I needed Jesus, and would never be happy without him.

In every life there are influences at work. We are not just physical and intellectual beings, we have a spiritual capacity too, but it is dormant, until God breathes his new life into us. Children are more spiritually perceptive than adults, and can, if the circumstances are right, receive this new life, unquestioningly, at an early age. But as we grow up we become hardened, wanting to go it alone. That was the case with me.

That time in Miami Beach when I knelt down in the church and repeated the prayer for salvation, I didn't understand what was happening but God took me at my word. From then onwards I belonged to him and though I wouldn't hand over to him, he followed me through the years, watching over me, letting me go my own way, till I was ready to turn to him for help, blessing and fulfilment.

He gives us a choice, all the time. If we choose to do his will, then life has a purpose, and a meaningful outcome. Most of my years I spent looking for that purpose, without knowing it. When I came to know Christ as someone who is real and alive, and living in power, I began to be the person I was meant to be.

In Joel 2, 25a it says, 'I will restore to you the years that the locusts have eaten. . . .' That is happening in my case. I have had as many and varied adventures since entering the Christian life, as I had before. Certainly I have visited as many countries, but this time with the satisfaction of leaving something permanent behind – a piece of knowledge about the God I serve.

He has used me in bringing others to know him. Sometimes I have merely been a link in the chain. One instance of this was conversation with a prostitute on the Hollywood Boulevard, in down town Los Angeles, during the 1984 Olympics. I was with the YWAM team, witnessing to the Olympic athletes, and to the crowds thronging to see the Games.

The prostitute was very young and pretty. She had left her husband in another city, to come and make a life for herself. But she had drifted into this sorry occupation because she could not otherwise earn a living. She flicked back her gold curls and said, 'I hope to get a break soon.'

I spent an hour telling her what the Lord had done in my life. 'Look,' I said, showing her an area on my leg where a malignant growth had been cut away three years ago, 'God has healed me. I could have lost my leg, but he has kept me well. He has provided the finances for me to come to L.A. to meet you. It's no coincidence that we are having this talk.'

She listened intently to all I said, and the next day, I heard later, committed her life to Christ when approached by another member of our team. When last heard of, she was going home to her husband.

As this book was being finished, Holiday on Ice came to Brighton, and Thelma and I went to see it. It was marvellous to watch Shirley-Marie playing badminton on ice, fast as ever, though Hugh Forgie was about to leave the show, handing over to his grandson. The act was being reformed, with a new look. What would become of Shirley-Marie? I told her that God had a plan for her life if she would only put her confidence in him. She smiled weakly, probably thinking, 'Another of Ann's crazy ideas.' I had so many of them in the old days, but this one is the best I've ever had.

Others were there that I knew. 'Come back and liven it up!' said Jean-Jacques, the dresser, whom I had known as a skater. I looked round the coffee bar where the cast were gathering in the interval and noticed that there were fewer English in the show, and that Czechs and Poles were predominant. There was another ice show on in London, and most of the English were there, with their Equity cards. I managed to see it and it was gorgeous, just like the old days. One difference was that they had a top class coach who encouraged up-and-coming young skaters, helping them to improve and move up the ladder.

In this country there is a great deal of interest in skating – for some reason we turn out excellent skaters all longing to emulate Torvill and Dean. This is miraculous when you consider that we have no Olympic-sized ice rinks, as they have in Europe, America and Canada, and indeed there is a chronic shortage of ice, including my home town. Local authorities don't see it as part of their responsibility to support officially home-grown skating talent. New leisure centres go up all over the country, but with no ice, yet skating is a good, clean sport, which the whole family can enjoy.

When skaters do show talent they have to sacrifice and fight for a place in the world's eye.

I owe skating a great deal. It gave me great opportunities I would not otherwise have had, and I grabbed them with both hands.

So I hope this book will encourage skaters to continue with their dream. If I have sounded critical of anything or anyone it is not to attack, but to tell of the experience of one struggling, adventurous girl, climbing the slippery stairway of fame, and hungry for life. To such a person out of the way things happen.

It never bothered me that I did not become a solo star. If skating had given me all my ambitions, I might have missed a greater glory.

As it is I know a love which transcends all human experience, and my ambition is to know Christ more day by day, and to learn to love others as he loves me.

THE TORN VEIL

Sister Gulshan and Thelma Sangster

Gulshan Fatima was brought up in a Muslim Sayed family according to the orthodox Islamic code of the Shias.

Suffering from a crippling paralysis she travelled to England in search of medical help. Although unsuccessful in medical terms, this trip marked the beginning of a spiritual awakening that led ultimately to her conversion to Christianity.

Gulshan and her father also travelled to Mecca in the hope that God would heal her, but that trip too was of no avail. However, Gulshan was not detered. She relentlessly pursued God and He faithfully answered her prayers. Her conversion, when it came, was dramatic and brought with a miraculous healing.

The Torn Veil is Sister Gulshan's thrilling testimony to the power of God which can break through every barrier.

RELEASE
The Miracle of the Siberian Seven

Timothy Chmykhalov with Danny Smith

The plight of the 'Siberian Seven' attracted widespread publicity and support.

Timothy Chmykhalov, youngest member of the seven, vividly recounts the events leading to the entry into the US Embassy in 1978, the long years of hoping and waiting, the uncertainty which faced them when they left in 1983 and finally the freedom which they found in America.

Release is a powerful testimony of faith and courage amidst intense pressure and threat of persecution. A story of hope and determination in the face of much discouragement.

NOW I CALL HIM BROTHER

Alec Smith

Alec Smith, son of Ian Smith the rebel Prime Minister of Rhodesia whose Unilateral Declaration of Independence plunged his country into twelve years of bloody racial war, has written his own story of those years.

The story of his life takes him from early years of rebellion against his role as 'Ian Smith's son' through his youth as a drop-out, hippy and drug peddler into the Rhodesian forces.

A dramatic Christian conversion experience at the height of the civil war transformed his life and led to the passionate conviction to see reconciliation and peace in a deeply divided country.

What follows is a thrilling account of how God can take a dedicated life and help to change the course of history.

OUT OF THE MELTING POT

Bob Gordon

Faith does not operate in a vacuum, it operates in human lives. God wants your life to be a crucible of faith.

Bob Gordon draws together Biblical principles and personal experience to provide valuable insights into this key area. Particular reference is made to the lessons he leant recently as God provided £600,000 to buy Roffey Place Christian Training Centre.

Out of the Melting Pot is Bob Gordon's powerful testimony to the work of God today and a profound challenge to shallow views of faith.

If you wish to receive *regular information* about *new books,* please send your name and address to:

London Bible Warehouse
PO Box 123
Basingstoke
Hants RG23 7NL

Name _____

Address _____

_____

_____

_____

I am especially interested in:
- [ ] Biographies
- [ ] Fiction
- [ ] Christian living
- [ ] Issue related books
- [ ] Academic books
- [ ] Bible study aids
- [ ] Children's books
- [ ] Music
- [ ] Other subjects

P.S. If you have ideas for new Christian Books or other products, please write to us too!